Biblical Theology for Beginners

Dan Carroll

For more information e-mail Water of Life Community Church at
info@wateroflifecc.org

Published by Water of Life Community Church
Fontana, California, U.S.A.
www.wateroflifecc.org
Printed in the U.S.A.

All Scripture quotations, unless otherwise indicated, are taken from the New American Standard Bible®, © 1960, 1962, 1963, 1968, 1971, 1972, 1973, 1975, 1977, 1995 by The Lockman Foundation. Used by permission.

Scripture quotations marked NLT are from the Holy Bible, New Living Translation, © 1996, 2004, 2007 by Tyndale House Foundation. Used by permission of Tyndale House Publishers, Inc., Carol Stream, Illinois 60188. All rights reserved.

Scripture quotations marked ESV are taken from the English Standard Version, © 2001. The ESV and English Standard Version are trademarks of Good News Publishers.

Scripture quotations marked KJV are taken from the Holy Bible, King James Version, 1611. Public domain.

Scripture quotations marked NIV are taken from the Holy Bible, New International Version®, NIV®, © 1973, 1978, 1984, by Biblica. Used by permission of Zondervan. All rights reserved worldwide.

Scripture quotations marked YLT are taken from the Holy Bible, Young's Literal Translation, 1898. Public domain.

New King James Version, © 1979, 1980, 1982 by Thomas Nelson, Inc. Used by permission. All rights reserved.

© 2010, 2014 Dan Carroll
All rights reserved
Second Edition
ISBN: 0-9913138-2-8

ISBN: 978-0-9913138-2-2

Library of Congress Control Number: 2010941415
Rights for publishing this book outside the U.S.A. or in non-English languages are administered by Water of Life Community Church. For additional information please visit www.wateroflifecc.org, e-mail info@wateroflifecc.org or write to Water of Life Community Church, 7625 East Avenue, Fontana, CA 92336, U.S.A.

Contents

Introduction 5

Part 1: Doctrinal Papers

1. The Doctrine of God..11
2. The Holy Spirit 17
3. The Incarnation..27
4. The Christology of Jesus 33
5. The Trinity 39
6. Creation 47
7. The Doctrine of Humankind 53
8. Evil and Sin 61
9. Christ and Salvation..67
10. The Atonement..75
11. The Assurance of Salvation 81
12. Justification 87
13. Regeneration/Sanctification 93
14. The Church 99
15. Baptism..107
16. The Lord's Supper 113
17. The Sacraments 119
18. Eschatology: The Return of Christ 125
19. Revelation..133
20. Providence 139
21. Scripture 147

Part 2: Position Papers

The Ministry and Gifts of the Holy Spirit 157
Appendix A: Spiritual Gifts 171
The Ministry and Gift of Prophecy 175
Appendix B: Functioning in the Gift of Prophecy 187
The Ministry and Gifts of Biblical Healing 189
Women in Leadership in the Church 205

Notes 219
Bibliography for "The Ministry and Gift of Prophecy" 221
Bibliography for "Women in Leadership in the Church" 223
About the Author 225
About Water of Life 227
Our Core Values 229

Introduction

This is a book about theology.

"But Pastor Dan, I'm not a theologian! And I don't want to study doctrine. I just want to follow Jesus."

I get it. The word *theology* sounds weighty. Daunting. Sometimes the thought of it spins my head too—and I went to seminary. But we all need to know some theology, or we will never grow in the full potential of our faith.

What is theology? According to Merriam-Webster's dictionary, theology simply means "the study of religious faith, practice, and experience: the study of God and God's relation to the world."

Theology is about answering questions and understanding the power of God in our lives. Do you want to know more about Him? How He works in your life? What about your purpose in life? Why did God create the world? Why do bad things happen to good people? Why do we pray? Is there a heaven and a hell? Does God heal? What does He think about women in ministry? How can the Holy Spirit live within us?

When it comes to serving God, there are thousands of questions. While this book doesn't answer all of them, it does provide a solid foundation for your faith. Knowing what we believe and how

God works equips us with answers. It opens up new vistas of faith and helps us relate to God in our everyday lives.

"That's awesome, Pastor Dan. I do want to know more about God. But isn't theology full of technical stuff like 'Herman newticks' and that other thing—'access Jesus' or something like that? It feels a little overwhelming. Can't I just read a book about God?"

It's called hermeneutics and exegesis. But you were close. Hermeneutics is a study of the methods of interpretation. Exegesis is a method of critical explanation of Scripture. But you're right—that's technical stuff. We won't get into either one too much. In this book we will stick to the basics. We will look at the practical and powerful aspects of how to live out what the Bible teaches.

Theology helps us in many ways. Second Timothy 2:15 tells us, "Be diligent to present yourself approved to God as a workman who does not need to be ashamed, accurately handling the word of truth." That's theology at work. It helps us handle the Word of truth—the Bible. And it helps us handle our lives.

First Peter 3:15 says, "Sanctify Christ as Lord in your hearts, always being ready to make a defense to everyone who asks you to give an account for the hope that is in you, yet with gentleness and reverence."

There was a time when it was easier to be a cultural Christian in our nation. We could come to faith and follow Christ without too many questions being asked and thus without needing too many answers. Nowadays, everyone asks not only the basic faith questions such as how can a good God let bad things happen to good people but also fundamental questions about miracles, the Bible and prayer. People even ask if we can prove that there is a God. Knowing what we believe and being ready to give an answer has become more important than ever. That's another way that knowing a little theology will help us in our everyday lives.

Second Peter 1:5 instructs us to "make every effort to respond to God's promises. Supplement your faith with a generous provision of moral excellence, and moral excellence with knowledge" (NLT).

Knowing the core tenets of what the Bible teaches and how we can apply them to our lives gives us a foundation in our walk with Christ. The more theology we know, the greater our grasp on how it all fits together.

A. W. Tozer once wrote, "Don't be satisfied with just reading the Word. Live the Word in power." Theology helps us see that we can come to the Bible expecting to find not only answers but God Himself speaking to us and empowering us.

Are you hungry for God to reveal Himself to you? I put this set of essays together when I was in seminary. They helped me as I relentlessly sought God's heart. Now I pray that you will allow the Holy Spirit to take you to new and deeper places. May God bless your journey of faith.

Pastor Dan

Part 1
Doctrinal Papers

1

The Doctrine of God

The doctrine of God, also known as theology proper, is the central point for a Christian's belief. Our view of God becomes the framework for all the rest of our theology. We could say that our doctrine of God will color everything else we believe. If we view God as a grandfather or a Santa Claus, we will certainly not fear Him as we ought, and likewise if we think of Him as a policeman, we will never know Him as a Father and a friend.

When we study the person of God, we study His attributes—the qualities that constitute who He is and the makeup of His nature—rather than His actions. Attributes, unlike actions, are permanent; they are neither gained nor lost. They make up the essence of who an individual is.

God Is Not Like Us

Many of God's attributes are unlike human ones. First, God is spirit and not flesh. He is not composed of matter, and thus is not limited to a physical body—even though He is described in Scripture as having hands and feet. These physical descriptors are simply what we call anthropomorphisms, or attempts to express who God is in terms that we humans can understand. Jesus was very clear about this: "God is spirit, and those who worship Him must worship in spirit and in truth" (John 4:24).

When we think of a spirit, we often confuse it with something that has no personality. That is not the case with God. Many other religions offer up a deity that is impersonal, but Christianity spells out the truth that God has a personality. If He didn't, He could not be personal with us. God has a name, which He indicated when He spoke to Moses: I AM. This name connotes far more of God's nature than our first glance at it may perceive. Throughout Scripture God's names help us understand His nature. They show us that God has feelings and thoughts, emotions and will. Each of these qualities makes up His personality.

Without these characteristics, our relationship with God would be defined much differently than it is. The Lord states in Exodus 20:2–3, "I am the LORD your God, who brought you out of the land of Egypt, out of the house of slavery. You shall have no other gods before Me." In this expression of who He is, we see God as someone who serves man and who also declares that man is to love and honor Him. Words such as these then define the boundaries of our relationship to Him.

God is alive. In fact, the Bible says that He is life. The very words *I AM* make this evident. This sets God apart from all other gods, which are merely objects. While people derive their life from Him, God does not get life from anywhere but Himself. He is eternal in life, meaning that His existence is not dependent on anything other than Himself.

God is by nature beyond our grasp. He is infinite, or unlimited and illimitable. This means that He is omnipresent—able to be at all places at all times—because He is not limited by space. He is immaterial and spiritual in nature.

He is at the same time always nearby, as we read in Jeremiah: "Am I a God at hand . . . and not a God far away?" (23:23, ESV). Psalm 139:7–12 asks if there is any place one can go out of the reach of God and then answers that there is none.

God is also not bound by time as we are; He is infinite in relation to time. God has always been, and He will always be. Psalm 90:1–2 states, "Lord, You have been our dwelling place in all generations. Before the mountains were born or You gave birth to the earth and the world, even from everlasting to everlasting, You are God."

Likewise, God's thoughts are immeasurable. His wisdom is beyond our ability to understand. "Great is our Lord and abundant in strength; His understanding is infinite" (Ps. 147:5). His wisdom is defined as His ability to always act in light of all the facts and to make judgments that are life-giving and perfect in every way. This is what the psalmist had in mind when he declared, "O LORD, how many are Your works! In wisdom You have made them all" (Ps. 104:24). Paul put it this way: "Oh, the depth of the riches both of the wisdom and knowledge of God! How unsearchable are His judgments and unfathomable His ways!" (Rom. 11:33).

Another of God's attributes that is so unlike humanity in its makeup is His constancy. God never changes! This is striking in a day and age in which so much is altered daily. Malachi 3:6 tells us of God, "I, the LORD, do not change." This offers a tremendous amount of security to those of us who love Him and are found in Him.

God's Moral Qualities

Much has been said of the attributes of God's greatness, but what of His goodness—His moral qualities? God's nature is bound to goodness and moral purity, which include holiness, righteousness, justice and faithfulness. What do these characteristics look like in God?

Holiness is often misunderstood; it seems so high and out of human reach. But simply stated, holiness is the perfection or the wholeness of God. Exodus 15:11 says, "Who is like You among the gods, O LORD? Who is like You, majestic in holiness, awesome in praises, working wonders?" To this question we can answer, "No one." God is unstained by evil and unblemished by wrong choices, as we see in Habakkuk 1:13: "Your eyes are too pure to approve evil, and You can not look on wickedness with favor."

God is also righteous, which means that He applies His goodness to His relationships. This literally means that God's actions are in accord with His attributes. He conducts Himself in the same manner in which He expects others to conduct themselves. God has established what is right in His law, which came out of His nature, so righteousness is therefore objective. He has also bound Himself to obeying what He has declared to be true and right. Righteousness is God's standard; it is internal and a part of His person. Thus, He walks consistently in it.

Justice is the third aspect of what we call God's moral qualities. We read earlier of God's law coming from His nature; justice is God's administering of that law to His creation, requiring it to conform to His law. This justice is bound to consequences as well. Romans 6:23 describes this well when it says, "The wages of sin is death." In order for God to be a just God, He must administer His law with integrity.

These are three areas of truth that are crucial in order for God to be holy. He must be genuine, or real about who He is and what He wants. He cannot trick mankind or in any other way deviate from being completely honest. He must function with veracity. In other words, God must say things the way they really are. He could fool us if He chose to, but He cannot do that and remain true to His nature. First Samuel 15:29 tells us that God cannot lie: "The Glory of Israel will not lie or change His mind; for He is not a man that He should change His mind." This means that God can always be trusted to tell us the whole truth.

Finally, the last aspect of God's moral character is His faithfulness, which actually means that He will not just *speak* truth but that He will prove to *be* true. Paul spoke of this in his first letter to the Thessalonian church: "Faithful is He who calls you, and He also will bring it to pass" (1 Thess. 5:24). The faithfulness of God is found throughout Scripture, as God repeatedly proves it by fulfilling His promises. From Abraham to Jesus, God keeps His promise.

God Is Love

Certainly God's attributes would be incomplete without stating that He is also love—not *loving* but *love*. In 1 John 4:8 we read that "God is love." The Bible states that love was first and foremost part of God's nature before it was ever something humans embraced. His love is unlike ours in that it is always unselfish, always benevolent and always kind. John 3:16 epitomizes this love when it cries out, "For God so loved the world, that He gave His only begotten Son, that whoever believes in Him shall not perish, but have eternal life."

God's mercy and His grace are the two key components of His love. His mercy is actually better understood by us as compassion. Matthew 14:14 speaks of Jesus seeing hurting and sick people and feeling compassion for them. God's grace declares that His love requires nothing of us and on the contrary flows completely out of God's nature and character. Ephesians 2:8–9 best describes this aspect of God's gift of love: "For by grace you have been saved through faith; and that not of yourselves, it is the gift of God; not as a result of works, so that no one may boast."

How we as humans respond to God and to His love toward us has always been a tension. On the one hand, God's holiness and justice demand that we honor Him. On the other hand, God's mercy and grace call us to intimacy and friendship with Him. The two issues before us require a balancing of God's immanence and His transcendence. God's immanence means that God is everywhere, in everything. Contrasting that is His transcendence, or His nature that is beyond our perception. If we focus too much on God's immanence, we are in danger of becoming too familiar with God. If we look too much at His transcendence, we can become too withdrawn from

Him and His awesomeness. We daily live in a tension between these two aspects of a living God, and we need to stay balanced between them.

It is through God's immanence that we come to know Him personally. Jesus said, "No longer do I call you slaves, for the slave does not know what His master is doing; but I have called you friends, for all things that I have heard from My Father I have made known to you" (John 15:15). But if God's transcendence is not kept in view as well, we are in constant danger of losing the perspective that God is God and that we are not. Isaiah 57:15 gives great balance to both aspects of God's nature:

> For thus says the high and exalted One who lives forever, whose name is Holy, "I dwell on a high and holy place, and also with the contrite and lowly of spirit in order to revive the spirit of the lowly and to revive the heart of the contrite."

Here is captured the glory of God. The Lord is high and holy, and yet He loves to draw near to those who call on His name and who believe in Him to heal them and renew life in them.

2

The Holy Spirit

The ministry of the Holy Spirit is, unfortunately, one of the most misunderstood teachings in Scripture. The ministry and personality of the Holy Spirit are often minimized as a doctrine and criticized as unnecessary for the Christian today. Often we are taught to fear the gifts and ministry of the Spirit as something out of the mainstream of our faith.

The truth is, in fact, the very opposite of these teachings. Without the empowering work of the Holy Spirit, we would be doomed to a spiritual life of frustration and disappointment. Without the inner working of the Spirit, we are destined to be unspiritual people.

The Holy Spirit is the third person of the godhead. As such, He fulfills several roles crucial to the believer's sanctification. However, His role as the third person of the Trinity has often been greatly misunderstood, and this misunderstanding has been the cause of a great deal of unwarranted strife in the body of Christ.

Is the Holy Spirit God?

There are a lot of commonly asked questions about the Holy Spirit: Is it acceptable or even allowable for a Christian to worship the Holy Spirit? Can a person's prayer be offered directly to the Holy Spirit? Is the Holy Spirit as much of the godhead as the Father and the Son? But before we explore these first two questions, it is crucial that we settle the third: the fact that the Spirit is just as much God as the Son and the Father are.

One of the clearest examples in the New Testament of this reality is seen in the story of Ananias and Sapphira. Peter, in confronting Ananias, declared,

> Ananias, why has Satan filled your heart to lie to the Holy Spirit and to keep back some of the price of the land? While it remained unsold, did it not remain your own? And after it was sold, was it not under your control? Why is it that you have conceived this deed in your heart? You have not lied to men but to God. (Acts 5:3–4)

Clearly, Peter interchanged the name of the Holy Spirit with that of God in this discourse. Paul did likewise in both 1 Corinthians 3:16–17 and 6:19–20. In the first instance Paul stated,

> Do you not know that you are a temple of God and that the Spirit of God dwells in you? If any man destroys the temple of God, God will destroy him, for the temple of God is holy, and that is what you are.

Paul obviously understood that being indwelt with the Holy Spirit is one and the same as being indwelt by God.

The Holy Spirit is often spoken of in the same sentence as the Father and the Son. We see this in Matthew 28:19, where Jesus references ministering the Great Commission "in the name of the Father and the Son and the Holy Spirit."

In order for each of the three distinct persons—the Father, the Son and the Holy Spirit—to be God, He must be:

> Eternal—always existent
> Omnipresent—always everywhere
> Omniscient—all knowing
> Omnipotent—all-powerful

So let's see if these qualities are true of the Holy Spirit. First, is the Holy Spirit eternal? Hebrews 9:14 declares that He is:

> How much more will the blood of Christ, who through the eternal Spirit offered Himself without blemish to God, cleanse your conscience from dead works to serve the living God?

Is He omnipresent? Psalm 139:7–10 provides the obvious answer:

> Where can I go from Your Spirit? Or where can I flee from Your presence? If I ascend to heaven, You are there; if I make my bed in Sheol, behold, You are there. If I take the wings of the dawn, if I dwell in the remotest part of the sea, even there Your hand will lead me, and Your right hand will lay hold of me.

Is the Holy Spirit all knowing, or omniscient? The Scriptures repeatedly say that He is:

> For to us God revealed them through the Spirit; for the Spirit searches all things, even the depths of God. For who among men knows the thoughts of a man except the spirit of the man which is in him? Even so the thoughts of God no one knows except the Spirit of God. (1 Cor. 2:10–11)

> But the Helper, the Holy Spirit, whom the Father will send in My name, He will teach you all things, and bring to your remembrance all that I said to you. (John 14:26)

> I have many more things to say to you, but you cannot bear them now. But when He, the Spirit of truth, comes, He will guide you into all the truth; for He will not speak on His own initiative, but whatever He hears, He will speak; and He will disclose to you what is to come. (John 16:12–13)

And fourth, is the Spirit all-powerful, or omnipotent? Yes, since He is spoken of as creator and the giver of life:

> You send forth Your Spirit, they are created; and You renew the face of the ground. (Ps. 104:30)

> But if the Spirit of Him who raised Jesus from the dead dwells in you, He who raised Christ Jesus from the dead will also give life to your mortal bodies through His Spirit who dwells in you. (Rom. 8:11)

Interacting with the Holy Spirit

Having thus established an initial defense for the deity of the Spirit, we can now begin answering the questions that were posed at the start of this chapter.

Is it acceptable for us to worship the Holy Spirit? The answer is certainly yes. As the third person of the godhead, the Holy Spirit deserves worship just as the Father and the Son do. Theoretically, we all worship Him every time we sing the Doxology:

> Praise God from whom all blessings flow,
> Praise Him all creatures here below,
> Praise Him above, ye heavenly hosts,
> Praise Father, Son, and Holy Ghost.

Interestingly enough, many so-called conservative evangelical believers think nothing of singing this song and offering worship to the Holy Spirit, but if they were asked if it is appropriate to worship the Spirit, they would often answer that it isn't.

Is it acceptable for us to pray to the Holy Spirit? Again, if the Spirit is in fact the Spirit of God, then the answer is most certainly yes. Though prayer isn't offered as regularly to the Spirit as it is to the Son and to the Father, there is no scriptural basis for directing prayer only to the Father and the Son.

Much of the misunderstanding on this issue arises from Jesus' discourse on the Spirit in John 16. It is here that He declared, "[The Spirit] will glorify me, for he will take what is mine and declare it to you" (16:14, ESV). Certainly, glorifying Jesus is a central focus of the ministry of the Spirit, but this in no way precludes the Spirit from operating in His role as One of the godhead.

The Holy Spirit: He or It?

Unfortunately, the use of the term *Holy Ghost* has over time stripped the Spirit of God of much of His personal effectiveness in many believers' lives. Is the Spirit a He, or is He an it? The Holy Spirit has a personality. He has knowledge, feelings and a will. This reality is found in both the Old and New Testaments. Here are a couple examples from Paul's writings:

> For to us God revealed them through the Spirit; for the Spirit searches all things, even the depths of God. For who among men knows the thoughts of

> a man except the spirit of the man which is in him? Even so the thoughts of God no one knows except the Spirit of God. (1 Cor. 2:10–11)

> In the same way the Spirit also helps our weakness; for we do not know how to pray as we should, but the Spirit Himself intercedes for us with groanings too deep for words; and He who searches the hearts knows what the mind of the Spirit is, because He intercedes for the saints according to the will of God. (Rom. 8:26–27)

The Greek word that references the Holy Spirit's mind in Romans 8:27 is *phronéma*. It contains the idea of knowledge, feeling and will combined. We see then that the Holy Spirit is indeed a person.

The Multifaceted Ministry of the Holy Spirit

Part of the problem that Christians face when dealing with the ministry of the Spirit is that His ministry is extremely varied. The Spirit functions in multiple roles.

He teaches us the heart of God:

> But the Helper, the Holy Spirit, whom the Father will send in My name, He will teach you all things, and bring to your remembrance all that I said to you. (John 14:26)

The Spirit also comforts us in our times of need:

> But I tell you the truth, it is to your advantage that I go away; for if I do not go away, the Helper will not come to you; but if I go, I will send Him to you. (John 16:7)

> Because you are sons, God has sent forth the Spirit of His Son into our hearts, crying "Abba! Father!" (Gal. 4:6)

And the Holy Spirit intercedes in prayer for us:

> In the same way the Spirit also helps our weakness; for we do not know how to pray as we should, but the Spirit Himself intercedes for us with groanings too deep for words; and He who searches the hearts knows what the mind of the Spirit is, because He intercedes for the saints according to the will of God. (Rom. 8:26–27)

When understood properly, these multifaceted roles that the Spirit plays in the Christian's life undergird the significant impact that the Holy Spirit intends to make as He builds spiritual men and women into the image of Jesus.

The Holy Spirit Empowers God's People

Clearly, without the power of the Spirit, spiritual maturity would be impossible for us. It is the Holy Spirit who empowers the believer to live. Let's look at how He does that.

Christians first receive the Holy Spirit at rebirth, according to Romans 8:9:

> You are not in the flesh but in the Spirit, if indeed the Spirit of God dwells in you. But if anyone does not have the Spirit of Christ, he does not belong to Him.

Yet this is only the initial sealing work of the Spirit, according to Ephesians 1:13. The empowering work of the Spirit, by which He gives the fruit of the Spirit, the gifts of the Spirit and the anointing of God, follows *after* we accept Christ as our Savior.

First, we receive the fruit of the Spirit. This is outlined in Galatians 5:22–23, which states that a believer who is walking in the Spirit will manifest certain qualities:

> The fruit of the Spirit is love, joy, peace, patience, kindness, goodness, faithfulness, gentleness, self-control; against such things there is no law.

Each of these fruits is borne out of a life that is daily lived in the power of the Holy Spirit, and they are a direct result of the sanctifying work of the Spirit within us.

Second, the Spirit imparts gifts to the believer. But in addition to being for our own personal growth, the gifts are intended for the edification of the whole body (see Rom. 12:3–8; 1 Cor. 12; Eph. 4:1–16; 1 Pet. 4:7–11).

The third impartation of the Spirit's life to us, the baptizing work of the Holy Spirit, is intended to empower the believer to serve and minister more effectively to those who are lost. Jesus declared as much in Acts 1:8:

> But you will receive power when the Holy Spirit has come upon you; and you shall be My witnesses both in Jerusalem, and in all Judea and Samaria, and even to the remotest part of the earth.

In summation, the work of the Spirit is crucial to all believers' spiritual maturity. One cannot be a spiritual person without the Holy Spirit. Without the Spirit we are powerless to impact the world for the kingdom of God. The "greater works" Jesus spoke of in John 14:12 could only take place, as He said in John 16:7, after He left the scene and the Holy Spirit arrived. Though tremendously misunderstood throughout the church's history, the work and ministry of the Spirit have continued to abound. More often than not, this has taken place in spite of the church's teachings, not because of them.

3
The Incarnation

God in a man. Stating incarnation in these terms may help us to understand why, historically speaking, the deity of Christ has been one of the most difficult theological topics to deal with. This particular subject is most often skewed when it is addressed by belief systems divergent from Christianity.

The deity of Jesus is far more crucial to our faith than we often acknowledge. The fact is, the whole of our belief in the work of salvation by grace rests upon this one test: was Jesus both man *and* God? He was, to be certain, the most extraordinary human being who has ever lived, but was He deity?

Jesus as God

Jesus Himself said, "He who has seen Me has seen the Father; how can you say, 'Show us the Father'?" (John 14:9). This tells us that we humans can indeed know the heart and person of God in Jesus. As a matter of fact, it declares that Jesus, as infinite God, the giver and sustainer of life, can come and redeem fallen mankind. It is in this God-man that mankind has been reunited with his creator, and so it is Jesus whom we worship as the creator and Savior of all.

The Scriptures speak volumes about Jesus' deity. Jesus made many assertions as to His identity that were clearly perceived by the Jews to be, in their terms, blasphemy. His claims, however, although clear, were never completely explicit. For example, He often forgave sins, which was an action that was certainly only God's prerogative. In Mark 2:5 Jesus declared to the paralytic, "Son, your sins are forgiven." When others were aghast at His words and questioned Him, He responded,

> "Why are you reasoning about these things in your hearts? Which is easier, to say to the paralytic, 'Your sins are forgiven'; or to say, 'Get up, and pick up your pallet and walk'? But so that you may know that the Son of Man has authority on earth to forgive sins"—He said to the paralytic, "I say to you, get up, pick up your pallet and go home." (2:8–11)

If His critics had been mistaken, Jesus could easily have corrected their assumption, but He didn't. He actually reiterated His statement to make clear to them that His action wasn't a mistake.

This circumstance was like many others that Jesus encountered during His ministry on Earth. Often He spoke of His transcendent power. He also claimed to be the judge of the entire world:

> But when the Son of Man comes in His glory, and all the angels with Him, then He will sit on His glorious throne. All the nations will be gathered before Him; and He will separate them from one another, as the shepherd separates the sheep from the goats; and He will put the sheep on His right, and the goats on the left. (Matt. 25:31–33)

This declaration left little room for people to doubt what He meant by His claims. Certainly Jesus avoided such assertions during the early years of His ministry, but just as certainly He offered no apology for stating them in His last year of ministry. For example, He told the Jews, "I and the Father are one" (John 10:30). Further, He claimed to be preexistent when He declared that He had existed before Abraham: "Jesus said to them, 'Truly, truly, I say to you, before Abraham was born, I am.' Therefore they picked up stones to throw at Him, but Jesus hid Himself and went out of the temple" (John 8:58–59).

One should make no mistake about the response Jesus received when He made such declarations. In the Jewish culture in which He lived, these claims were blasphemy. In the Jews' eyes Jesus was making Himself out to be God, and it was for that reason that they picked up stones to stone Him. This all came into clear focus during Jesus' trial when He was accused by many of these same Pharisees of having "made himself the Son of God" (John 19:7, ESV).

In Matthew 26:63–66 we find further evidence of the Jews' feelings when we read of the high priest condemning Jesus:

> The high priest said to Him, "I adjure You by the living God, that You tell us whether You are the Christ, the Son of God." Jesus said to him, "You have said it yourself; nevertheless I tell you, hereafter you will see the Son of Man sitting at the right hand of Power, and coming on the clouds of heaven." Then the high priest tore his robes and said, "He has blasphemed! What further need do we have of witnesses? Behold, you have now heard the blasphemy; what do you think?" They answered, "He deserves death!"

Rather than deny the charge, Jesus built on the words of the priest, stating that He was indeed the Son of Man and that He would be seated on the throne of God. And so Jesus was in fact crucified for making the claim that He was God in flesh.

Following Jesus' crucifixion and resurrection, we find more evidence of Jesus claiming to be deity when Thomas saw Him and declared, "My Lord and my God!" (John 20:28). Not only did Jesus not try to dissuade Thomas, He received his praise.

Likewise, Paul offered ample defense of Christ's deity throughout his writings. Colossians 1:15 states, "He is the image of the invisible God." And later in chapter 2 of the same book, Paul states as clearly as he could possibly say, "For in Him all the fullness of Deity dwells in bodily form" (2:9). Further, Paul explains in Philippians 2:5–11 Jesus' preexistence and His transformation into bodily form, stating, "Although He existed in the form of God, [He] did not regard equality with God a thing to be grasped, but emptied Himself, taking the form of a bond-servant, and being made in the likeness of men" (2:6–7).

Jesus as Man

Having made a clear biblical case for the deity of Christ, we now turn to the truth regarding His humanity. Was Jesus really human, and how important is it to establish the credibility of His humanity? First, for Jesus to be able to offer Himself as a sacrifice for mankind, it was crucial for Him to be one of us. In Christ we have both God and man. In Him we have a glimpse of what humanity was meant to be. We see how we were originally created to be before the Fall.

Beginning with Jesus' birth, we see that Jesus was in all ways like us. He traveled the birth canal to enter the world, and He lay in a grave when He left. He was conceived in a human womb, and He struggled as we do to grow and mature: "And Jesus kept increasing in wisdom and stature, and in favor with God and men" (Luke 2:52). Jesus wasn't born totally mature, nor was He born without the limitations that come with being human. He experienced hunger, tiredness and thirst as we do (see John 4:6; 19:28; Matt. 4:2).

Jesus was saddled with human emotions that were difficult for Him to deal with at times (see Matt. 26:37–38). He felt sorrow, pain and heartache when He interacted with humanity. He felt compassion and trouble in His spirit as well as deep love for others. Nowhere do we see the wide range of Jesus' emotions more clearly than we do when Lazarus died:

> When Jesus therefore saw her weeping, and the Jews who came with her also weeping, He was deeply moved in spirit and was troubled, and said, "Where have you laid him?" They said to Him, "Lord, come and see." Jesus wept. So the Jews were saying, "See how He loved him!" (John 11:33–36)

Paul spoke of Jesus being "manifested in the flesh" (1 Tim. 3:16, ESV) and also clarified the need for Jesus to be both fully human and fully God: "There is one God, and one mediator also between God and men, the man Christ Jesus" (1 Tim. 2:5). Paul's use of the term *man* is significant in that he assumed the need for Jesus to be both God and man in order for Him to heal the broken relationship between God and man.

How then do these two natures work out in the person of Jesus? This has been and continues to remain one of the most difficult theological issues the church has faced. How could Jesus be God and not know all things? Or how could He be human and never sin or fall into temptation? Philippians 2:6–7 holds the answer to most of these questions: "Although He existed in the form of God, [He] did not regard equality with God a thing to be grasped, but emptied Himself, taking the form of a bond-servant, and being made in the likeness of men."

This passage describes what is called kenosis—Jesus being emptied of His divine attributes. Jesus existed in the form of God before He came to Earth and then took on the form of a bondservant. We are not told that Jesus stopped existing as God, only that He divested Himself not of divinity but of the equality that He had as part of the godhead and took on the form of humanity. When He did this, Jesus did not cease to have the nature of God, but that nature was now poured into the frailty of humanity.

Nor did Jesus function as One with dual natures. He functioned as One who was fully human and fully deity. This can best be illustrated by a look at God's original intent for mankind before the Fall. When we think of Jesus functioning as God in flesh, we are often bound by the concept we have of flesh. It is corrupt and fallen, it is weak and sinful, and it is hopeless and hurting. But prior to the Fall, this was not the case with either Adam or Eve. Both of them were much more whole than we can imagine. They were in the image of God and without blemish or imperfection. This is much closer to what Jesus' humanity looked like than ours.

Jesus' incarnation gives us the defining picture that many of us need of our heavenly Father's heart. Jesus is God in the flesh. His love for people, His compassion and kindness, His willingness to suffer—all these unfold the Father's heart for those of us who hunger for more of Him. They allow us, they beckon for us, to draw near to God and to find Him to be beyond our wildest dreams: a God who is in love with us, His people.

4
The Christology of Jesus

The word *Christology* is derived from two Greek words, *Christos* and *logos*. This compound word is used in theology to describe the person and work of Jesus Christ. Christology is a study of the defining aspects of Scripture as they pertain to Jesus being the Messiah, the chosen One of God.

The Virgin Birth

When studying the Christology of Jesus, we must begin with the virgin birth. This unparalleled event that was prophesied by Isaiah is certainly a defining point in the Messiah's journey. It is here that the theological battles have been historically fought.

The arguments regarding the virgin birth have taken several interesting twists throughout history. First, was Jesus' conception an immaculate one? Second, is it even crucial that Jesus' birth be an immaculate conception? Is there ample information to defend such a doctrine? What does it mean if Jesus' conception wasn't "of the Holy Spirit" (Matt. 1:20)?

The Bible contains two explicit references to the virgin birth. (The phrase *virgin birth*, it should be noted, is not accurate terminology. In reality, when we speak of the biblical accounts of Mary and the baby Jesus, we are speaking not of a virgin birth but of a virgin conception.) These two accounts offer differing information, although they certainly don't contradict each other. The Matthew account states,

> Now the birth of Jesus Christ was as follows: when His mother Mary had been betrothed to Joseph, before they came together she was found to be with child by the Holy Spirit. And Joseph her husband, being a righteous man and not wanting to disgrace her, planned to send her away secretly. But when he had considered this, behold, an angel of the Lord appeared to him in a dream, saying, "Joseph, son of David, do not be afraid to take Mary as your wife; for the Child who has been conceived in her is of the Holy Spirit. She will bear a Son; and you shall call His name Jesus, for He will save His people from their sins." Now all this took place to fulfill what was spoken by the Lord through the prophet: "Behold, the virgin shall be with child and shall bear a Son, and they shall call His name Immanuel," which translated means, "God with us." And Joseph awoke from his sleep and did as the angel of the Lord commanded him, and took Mary as his wife, but kept her a virgin until she gave birth to a Son; and he called His name Jesus. (1:18–25)

This text offers a clear and defining account of Jesus' conception by stating not once but twice that His would, quite literally, be a miraculous conception. We see in verse 18 that Mary was with child "by the Holy Spirit," and we see again in verse 20 that the angel revealed to Joseph that this child was supernatural: "The child who has been conceived in her is of the Holy Spirit." This is an obvious attempt on Matthew's part to indicate that Jesus' conception was a miraculous event that superseded anything God had done before in the birthing of a child.

Unfortunately, some have chosen to discount these foundational facts because they reason that these statements are not made at any other point in Scripture. But the fact that the account in Matthew incorporates the Old Testament prophetic announcement found in the Immanuel prophecies of Isaiah certainly gives an authoritative sense of reason and purpose in this passage as well.

Like so many of the theological battles the church has fought during its history, this one is often driven not by biblical accounts but by extra-biblical and mystical additions that have been given to the story by the Catholic church. The Catholic position has not only elevated Jesus' mother Mary to near deity, but it has clouded the air concerning the actual facts that the Bible offers surrounding the virgin birth. Many Catholics interpret the virgin birth as meaning that Jesus never entered the birth canal but that He instead miraculously passed through the wall of Mary's uterus as well as her stomach and was thus birthed supernaturally. Additionally, they propagate the myth that Mary never engaged in sexual intercourse, even after Jesus' birth (as if the act of intercourse would have made her less than holy), and that she had no natural children. This, in turn, caused them to find a way to redefine those whom Scripture describes as Jesus' brothers, whom they conveniently call His cousins. As it has with many other doctrines in the New Testament, this kind of folklore has done more to disrupt the beauty and the truth of the Scriptures than to enhance the greatness of God.

The fact that Jesus was rumored in New Testament times to be illegitimate actually lends credence to the truth of His immaculate conception. We encounter this perception in John 8:41, where the Jews declared to Jesus, "*We* were not born of fornication; we have one Father: God" (emphasis added). This was clearly a reference on their part to Jesus' questionable ancestry.

The fact that there are not more obvious mentions of Jesus' birth in New Testament Scripture does seem to be problematic for some. The Gospel accounts of Mark and John both have glaring omissions here, as do the book of Acts and Paul's writings.

The Gospel account of Mark actually lacks several of the narrative stories found in both Matthew's and Luke's Gospels. It seems to incorporate only the public accounts of Jesus' ministry and none of the private narrative found in Matthew and Luke. What Mark does do in his account is offer a very good hint at the possibility that he did in fact know of Jesus' virgin birth. We see this in his account of people asking if Jesus was not the carpenter's son:

> "Where did this man get these things, and what is this wisdom given to Him, and such miracles as these performed by His hands? Is not this the carpenter, the son of Mary, and brother of James and Joses and Judas and Simon? Are not His sisters here with us?" And they took offense at Him. (Mark 6:2–3)

It appears that Mark took great pains in this account not to mention Jesus having an earthly father. This is a strange thing for a writer in a Jewish culture to do, seeing that a Jewish male's ancestry was always traced through his father's side of the family and not the mother's. Yet Mark mentions only Jesus' mother.

As for the writings in the balance of the New Testament, it is obvious that the virgin birth was not an issue. This may have been because it was never challenged. Most of the issues Paul wrote on were those challenged by others or that primarily centered around evangelism and the building of the church.

The Implications of the Virgin Birth

How important is it that Jesus' birth was a virgin birth? What implications does a virgin birth have on the balance of our faith? First, Jesus' virgin birth is a critical reminder to us that all God does is supernatural. The prophetic account of Jesus found in Isaiah 9:6–7 pronounces this a fact:

> For a child will be born to us, a son will be given to us; and the government will rest on His shoulders; and His name will be called Wonderful Counselor, Mighty God, Eternal Father, Prince of Peace. There will be no end to the increase of His government or of peace, on the throne of David and over His kingdom, to establish it and to uphold it with justice and righteousness from then on and forevermore. The zeal of the LORD of hosts will accomplish this.

Jesus' name was to be called wonderful, *pehleh*, or in our terms today "wonder-filled." This word *wonderful* is not an adjective describing the noun *counselor*; it is a noun describing the person of Jesus, whom we are told in Isaiah 7:14 would be conceived supernaturally. Jesus' whole life was marked by this prophetic announcement. His life was truly "wonder-filled." It was characterized by the miracles He performed and the pronouncements and teachings He brought, in which He declared that the kingdom of God was at hand.

Further, the virgin birth points us to the reality that humans do not have the power or the possibility of salvation outside the ministry of the Holy Spirit, for as the Holy Spirit birthed life in Mary, so He births life in those who believe in the Son of God as the Savior. This is the work of the Messiah, the Savior—to impart new life to those who are dead and dying from the effects of sin (see Rom. 6:23). This supernatural work reminds us that God's grace is a miraculous gift, as was the supernatural impartation of the child to Mary.

Finally, the virgin birth reflects the historical work of God among His people to work in miraculous ways to birth children of destiny. He did this repeatedly throughout the Old and New Testaments with such people as Samuel, Isaac and John the Baptist as well as with Sarah and Abram when He asked them, "Is anything too difficult for the LORD?" (Gen. 18:14). The virgin birth loudly answers no!

So we see that the virgin birth points directly to all that Jesus was and is to be for His people. It is the foundational and defining aspect of His Christology.

5

The Trinity

The doctrine that sets the Christian faith apart from all other world religions—the one doctrine that is truly and totally distinctive to Christianity—is the doctrine of the Trinity. That there is one God with three distinct functioning persons makes Christianity a faith set apart from all others. Christianity is a faith in the triune God.

This statement itself reflects the difficulty of dealing with this seemingly contradictory doctrine. To complicate matters more, nowhere in the Scriptures do we find an explicit statement regarding the doctrine of the Trinity, yet this doctrine has been in the language of Christians from the beginning of the church.

God Is One

In order for us to understand the doctrine of the Trinity, we must examine the foundations of our faith. The historical background of Christianity is certainly Judaism. It is here that we find that God is one, not three. Monotheism is crucial to the Judeo-Christian faith. Yet just as true is the fact that without a Trinitarian belief, Christianity is not Christianity. One may attempt to make a case otherwise, but if Jesus isn't God, then much if not all of Christianity is not acceptable.

Beginning in the Old Testament, monotheism is clearly taught. We see this truth firmly established in Exodus 20:2–3 with the deliverance of the Ten Commandments: "I am the LORD your God, who brought you out of the land of Egypt, out of the house of slavery. You shall have no other gods before Me." This prohibition of any other gods demonstrates for time and eternity that God is, as He said, Lord and that He alone is to be worshiped as God. The book of Deuteronomy builds on this belief by declaring that this teaching of monotheism should be to the Hebrew first and foremost:

> Hear, O Israel! The LORD is our God, the LORD is one! You shall love the LORD your God with all your heart and with all your soul and with all your might. These words, which I am commanding you today, shall be on your heart. You shall teach them diligently to your sons and shall talk of them when you sit in your house and when you walk by the way and when you lie down and when you rise up. You shall bind them as a sign on your hand and they shall be as frontals on your forehead. You shall write them on the doorposts of your house and on your gates. (Deut. 6:4–9)

The New Testament follows the same pattern of monotheism. James tells us, "You believe that God is one. You do well; the demons also believe, and shudder" (2:19). The apostle Paul repeatedly reinforces this belief with statements interwoven throughout his teaching on other issues. One such statement is found in 1 Corinthians 8:4–6, which obviously declares the oneness of God:

> Therefore concerning the eating of things sacrificed to idols, we know that there is no such thing as an idol in the world, and that there is no God but one.

> For even if there are so-called gods whether in heaven or on earth, as indeed there are many gods and many lords, yet for us there is but one God, the Father, from whom are all things and we exist for Him; and one Lord, Jesus Christ, by whom are all things, and we exist through Him.

Jesus as a Member of the Trinity

Having identified the truth of a monotheistic faith, where does that leave the Christian who is unable to find any explicit statement about a triune God? It is already clear that the Father is God. This issue is not in dispute, nor has it ever been a point of major contention, but what of the other two members of this triune godhead? Both are certainly more problematic for our discussion.

The deity of Jesus has been a contentious issue for many. But, as we discussed at length in the previous chapter, the Scriptures speak volumes concerning Jesus' deity. Jesus made many assertions that were perceived by the Jews to be, in their terms, blasphemies. His claims though were never totally explicit. He forgave sins, an action that was clearly believed to be only God's prerogative. We see in Mark 2:5 that Jesus declared, "Son, your sins are forgiven." When others were aghast at His words and questioned Him in verse 7, He responded in verses 8–11:

> "Why does this man speak that way? He is blaspheming; who can forgive sins but God alone?" Immediately Jesus, aware in His spirit that they were reasoning that way within themselves, said to them, "Why are you reasoning about these things in your hearts? Which is easier, to say to the paralytic, 'Your sins are forgiven'; or to say, 'Get up, and pick up your pallet and walk'? But so that you may know that

the Son of Man has authority on earth to forgive sins"—He said to the paralytic, "I say to you, get up, pick up your pallet and go home."

Had Jesus wanted to, He could have easily corrected their mistaken assumption, but He didn't. In fact, He reiterated His statement to make sure that they understood this wasn't a mistake. In the book of John, He was as overt as He would ever be about His deity when He stated, "He who has seen Me has seen the Father; how can you say, 'Show us the Father'?" (14:9). This declaration seems to put Jesus on an equal plane with the Father.

Paul supports this position with his teaching in Colossians 1:15–20. He states, "He is the image of the invisible God" (1:15). And later in chapter 2 of the same book, he reiterates with a statement as defining as we will find in the New Testament: "For in Him all the fullness of Deity dwells in bodily form" (2:9).

In Philippians 2:5–7 Paul affirms Christ's deity in what is the New Testament's most compelling statement on the second person of the godhead, stating,

> Have this attitude in yourselves which was also in Christ Jesus, who, although He existed in the form of God, did not regard equality with God a thing to be grasped, but emptied Himself, taking the form of a bond-servant, and being made in the likeness of men.

We do not have a more thorough theological statement regarding Jesus' deity—and this from a Hebrew who knew well the need for Christians to worship one God and one God alone. Jesus, we are told, "existed in the form of God," and He didn't "regard equality with God a thing to be grasped." For Paul, a Hebrew, trained as a

Pharisee, to have made such a statement without believing that he was calling Jesus God pushes the boundaries of reason. If Jesus is equal with God, then He must be God; and if there is only one God, then there must be a mystery unfolding here that will stretch the human capacity to embrace and understand it.

Jesus actually helped define the perimeters of the doctrine of a triune God when He claimed to be preexistent, declaring that He had existed before Abraham:

> Jesus said to them, "Truly, truly, I say to you, before Abraham was born, I am." Therefore they picked up stones to throw at Him, but Jesus hid Himself and went out of the temple. (John 8:58–59)

The Holy Spirit as a Member of the Trinity

But what of the Holy Spirit's place as the third person of the godhead? There are no such statements in Scripture as clear as the ones pertaining to Jesus. What we do have are multiple inferences of the Holy Spirit's role in the Trinity. The earliest and probably the clearest is found in Acts 5:3–4, when Ananias and Sapphira lie about the property they have sold:

> Peter said, "Ananias, why has Satan filled your heart to lie to the Holy Spirit and to keep back some of the price of the land? While it remained unsold, did it not remain your own? And after it was sold, was it not under your control? Why is it that you have conceived this deed in your heart? You have not lied to men but to God."

We can see that for Peter, lying to the Holy Spirit was likened to and considered the same as lying to God. Paul seems to be comfortable making the same comparison in 1 Corinthians 3:16–17 when he mingles the name for God and for the Holy Spirit: "Do you not know that you are a temple of God and that the Spirit of God dwells in you? If any man destroys the temple of God, God will destroy him, for the temple of God is holy, and that is what you are."

When the Old Testament is closely examined, one discovers that what Paul and Peter have done is not exclusive to their beliefs but is actually founded in their Hebraic backgrounds. In Genesis 1:26 we see that God says, "Let Us make man in Our image, according to Our likeness; and let them rule over the fish of the sea and over the birds of the sky and over the cattle and over all the earth, and over every creeping thing that creeps on the earth." Using the plural form in "let Us make" and "in Our image" opens the door for the doctrine of the Trinity.

There are other examples of the plural nouns being used in describing God. Isaiah 6:8 offers one such: "Then I heard the voice of the Lord, saying, 'Whom shall I send, and who will go for Us?' Then I said, 'Here am I. Send me!'" Had these declarations not been made in this way, there is little chance that either Peter or Paul would have chosen to freely interchange the expressions of the Holy Spirit and God.

The New Testament seems to strengthen the case for a Trinitarian view by linking the three persons of the godhead together in a unity that supports equality. Jesus did this in Matthew 28:19: "Go therefore and make disciples of all the nations, baptizing them in the name of the Father and the Son and the Holy Spirit." That Jesus used a singular form for *name* and then listed three persons infers that each person is a part of the godhead. Paul more than once did the same. In 2 Corinthians 13:14 he wrote, "The grace of the Lord Jesus Christ, and the love of God, and the fellowship of the Holy Spirit, be with you all." The Gospel of John likewise does this, offering a glimpse at the inter-dynamics of the godhead:

> I will ask the Father, and He will give you another Helper, that He may be with you forever; that is the Spirit of truth, whom the world cannot receive, because it does not see Him or know Him, but you know Him because He abides with you and will be in you. (John 14:16–17)

Here we have Jesus asking, the Father responding and the Holy Spirit answering.

In conclusion, it is clear that Scripture teaches that there is one God and that He consists of three persons: the Father, the Son and the Holy Spirit. The deity of each person must be affirmed, and the equality of the three must be maintained. They are each qualitatively the same—they are all eternal. One or more of them were not added later. There has never been an alteration of God, yet He has functioned throughout history, and He continues to function today, to achieve different ends through the differing roles and different persons of the godhead.

6
Creation

One of the greatest works of God must certainly be His creation. Not only is it amazingly grand—so much so that many worship it instead of Him—but God's creation holds many keys to a life-giving perspective of Christianity. Unfortunately, with today's rapidly unfolding scientific research, there seems to be a constant tension between the church and science that tends to marginalize the magnificence of all that God has done.

The doctrine of creation is essential to Christianity in that it undergirds and sustains the Christian's belief that everything derives its existence from God. This truth is fundamental to the belief that there is no reality except that which God has created. Christianity believes that God created something out of nothing. No other matter previously existed, as dualism contends; there was no other reality that God mixed His material with in order to create the world. On the contrary, God created something out of the nothing that He chose to create with. He created raw material and endowed it with His identity so that it would reflect Him and His character to mankind.

God Saw That It Was Good

Thus affirming that God alone created matter and endowed it with His character, we can state that all creation is good, because God is good and therefore would not create anything intrinsically evil.

This is something that the Bible speaks a great deal about. In Genesis 1 we see God declaring that what He had made was good:

> God called the dry land earth, and the gathering of the waters He called seas; and God saw that it was good. . . . The earth brought forth vegetation, plants yielding seed after their kind, and trees bearing fruit with seed in them, after their kind; and God saw that it was good. . . . God made the two great lights, the greater light to govern the day, and the lesser light to govern the night; He made the stars also. God placed them in the expanse of the heavens to give light on the earth, and to govern the day and the night, and to separate the light from the darkness; and God saw that it was good. . . . God created the great sea monsters and every living creature that moves, with which the waters swarmed after their kind, and every winged bird after its kind; and God saw that it was good. . . . God made the beasts of the earth after their kind, and the cattle after their kind, and everything that creeps on the ground after its kind; and God saw that it was good. (Gen. 1:10, 12, 16–18, 21, 25)

This fact, if dealt with honestly, brings us face to face with the question of evil: if God created everything, and it was all good, then how did evil enter the world?

Dualism contends that this problem is simply resolved by assuming that in His creation of the world, God used some material that already existed, and it was that matter that was intrinsically evil. The doctrine of creation answers that claim with the declaration that evil's entrance into the world is the responsibility of man. The existence of evil has nothing to do with the physical world being evil in itself but with man possessing a free will and having used it in such a way that he and he alone is responsible for sin and evil in the world.

Though evil may manifest in society, that is not society's fault. Evil may manifest in physical and even sexual ways, yet this does not mean that physical and sexual things are inherently bad, as the church has sometimes led us to believe throughout history. This propensity for asceticism—the shunning of physical things in the name of God—has left many wondering how God could have created such wonderful things, declaring that they were good, and yet prohibit Christians from enjoying them.

Most importantly, we find in the doctrine of creation the truth that there is a God, and He is not man. Although man is certainly creative, having been made in the image of God who is the creator, man cannot create out of nothing as God did, nor is everything man creates good. Man has inherent limitations, limitations that God does not possess; therefore he will never be equal to God. Man was, of course, created above the animals and in the image of God, but he should never be worshiped, for worship, as we are told in the Scriptures, is intended for God and God alone.

Some Questions About Creation

How did God create? The church has held that He created *ex nihilo*, or out of nothing. Creation has been, we are told in Mark 13:19, "since the beginning of the creation which God created." There was no preexistent matter. Paul tells us the same in Romans 4:17: "God . . . gives life to the dead and calls into being that which does not exist." God, Genesis 1 tells us, simply spoke the world into existence (see Gen. 1:3, 6, 9).

The next question we have to address is the question of whether or not God actually created all of existence or merely the part we comprehend. The Bible tells us that He created it all: "O Lord, it is You who made the heaven and the earth and the sea, and all that is in them" (Acts 4:24). "The God who made the world and all things in it, since He is Lord of heaven and earth, does not dwell in temples made with hands" (17:24).

What was God's purpose in creating this world? Psalm 19:1 tells us simply that all creation brings glory to Him: "The heavens are telling of the glory of God; and their expanse is declaring the work of His hands."

Science and the Bible

Today the great conflict rages between science and the Bible. This, we know, is a relatively new battle. Prior to the 1800s, geology was an undeveloped science. It wasn't until Darwinism and science developed that we began to encounter the prolific battles we see today between science and creationism.

It is this author's contention that the Bible is not a science book, and it was never meant to be. It does, however, give deep glimpses at scientific things as it does toward most spheres of life. The Bible is a book on life—how God gave life to men and how He continues to try to impart it to us through a life-giving relationship with Him.

The Bible's primary emphasis is on what God did and why He did it and the implications of His actions for mankind. It does give credence to how He did it, but that certainly isn't the crux of the matter. When we try to get into the hows of creation, the waters get murky. There are several opinions or theories that have been offered over the years. They are primarily found in two categories: the young-earth theory and the old-earth theory.

One of the young-earth theories, the ideal-time theory, contends that God made the earth in a six-day period a short time ago but that He made it to look as if it were billions of years old. Another young-earth theory is that the flood of Noah was used by God to accomplish thousands of years of transformation in a short period of time. This theory contends that the water flooding the earth was under immense pressure that accomplished unusual events in a short amount of time.

Some old-earth proponents have adopted a view that is known as theistic evolution. According to this view, God began the process of evolution at creation and has worked within its framework ever since. A similar theory called progressive creationism holds that God created everything in a series of acts over a long period of time, and, consequently, it took a long time for the earth to develop. In other words, He made each animal and then allowed for evolution to continue the process of creating over time.

God's Purpose in Creation

We will not attempt to answer the question of how in the brevity of this paper, however, as much as we will seek answers to our primary question: why. Why is it crucial that God created?

If we are assured that God created all things and that everything He made is good, we are actually saying that all things have value. Consequently, rather than holding that God gave dominion to mankind at creation so that we could pillage and destroy, as some Christians have contended, we should see our dominion as stewardship of God's good creation, as we are told in Revelation 4:11, and recognize the blessing that everything God made holds for all mankind.

The fact that God created everything and declared that it is good should give us balance in our daily living. We are fully spiritual, mental, emotional and physical people, and He created us to be so. This is all good in God's eyes.

Finally, the fact that science finds a rhyme and reason to creation should help us know that God did create with a logical pattern in mind. Nothing is haphazard, but everything has an intelligent direction and design to it. We can rest assured that all science will do, as it further discovers different aspects concerning creation, is verify what the Bible has already declared to be true. As a result, we can rest in His greatness to make something out of nothing and to form a way when there is no way. As the psalmist says in Psalm 77:13–14, "What god is great like our God? You are the God who works wonders."

7

The Doctrine of Humankind

The doctrine of man is an interesting and vitally crucial topic, particularly in today's world. It seems as if everyone has an answer for the question of mankind's purpose and destiny in this life. The search for purpose and meaning in today's scientific and technically intense environment is so strong that we can almost hear the cry of people's hearts for something tangible and life-giving—something that goes beyond intellect and touches their spirits.

Man has traveled to the moon and engineered incredible scientific feats, many of which had never been dreamed possible, yet at the same time he seems unable or unwilling to control himself. The doctrine of man attempts to make sense out of this dilemma. If people are made in the image of God and thus belong to Him, then this reality has profound repercussions for how we live and what we value. If Jesus is the full revelation of what God intended man to be, then this should impact how we view ourselves and those around us. Finally, if we are made in the image of God, then we must have need of relationship with God.

The above concerns have tremendous implications, both morally and ethically, for all mankind. For those of us who believe that Jesus Christ is the salvation of the world, these issues must be clearly understood, or we will never be effective in touching others and building God's kingdom. The truth is that if we don't have a solid grasp of the certainty of these matters, it is nearly impossible for us to develop a philosophy of ministry for serving God's people. Simply put, if we are created in God's image, then we are people of destiny; but if we are no different than the animals, we are not. These issues thrust us back into the Scriptures in search of God's view of His highest creation—mankind.

What Is Man, and Why Did God Make Him?

Does God view man as a machine? The answer is no. But we do at times. When we view people as machines, we treat them as objects, and we attempt to satisfy their needs in order to keep them producing.

Does God view mankind as another part of His animal kingdom? Again, the answer is no. Even though much of science today does view man as a complex form of animal, this perspective degrades humanity and undermines the dignity and ethical possibility of people. It understands people in terms of their biological drives and little else.

Is man just a sexual being, as Freud proposed, or an economic and material being consumed with meeting his primary needs of food, clothing and shelter? Once again, the answer is no. If man is viewed or views himself in any of these terms, he will ultimately find that there is still a well of emptiness and dissatisfaction within him that he has failed to address.

God created man in His image, and that knowledge is critical to our wellbeing. We were created as eternal beings, not merely physical and material ones. Our value was conferred on us by our creator, and as a result, we are only fulfilled in relationship to that creator. As such, personal satisfaction comes only when we give in to God's purposes. Jesus put it this way: "Whoever wishes to save his life will lose it, but whoever loses his life for My sake and the gospel's will save it. For what does it profit a man to gain the whole world, and forfeit his soul?" (Mark 8:35–36).

The Bible teaches that God, our creator, is intimately acquainted with all our ways and that we are very special to Him. As David so clearly states,

> What is man that You take thought of him, and the son of man that You care for him? Yet You have made him a little lower than God, and You crown him with glory and majesty! You make him to rule over the works of Your hands; You have put all things under his feet. (Ps. 8:4–6)

Jesus said that each individual was not only significant to God but worth pursuing: "What man among you, if he has a hundred sheep and has lost one of them, does not leave the ninety-nine in the open pasture and go after the one which is lost until he finds it?" (Luke 15:3–4).

In order to establish the foundation of this truth, however, we must go to the origin of mankind. In Genesis 1:26–28 we see God making mankind and establishing him in His presence:

> Then God said, "Let Us make man in Our image, according to Our likeness; and let them rule over the fish of the sea and over the birds of the sky and over the cattle and over all the earth, and over every creeping thing that creeps on the earth." God created man in His own image, in the image of God He created him; male and female He created them. God blessed them; and God said to them, "Be fruitful and multiply, and fill the earth, and subdue it; and rule over the fish of the sea and over the birds of the sky and over every living thing that moves on the earth."

In Genesis 2:7 we see God specifically setting the spark of life in man with His breath of life: "Then the LORD God formed man of dust from the ground, and breathed into his nostrils the breath of life; and man became a living being." Both of these accounts in Genesis help us glimpse the magnitude of intimacy that God intended to have with people as His creation.

Unfortunately, many disregard this account as a fairy tale intended to enhance the story of life found in the Scriptures. But what does the Bible say about Adam and Eve? Were they real characters, or were they fictitious symbols meant to represent a sense of what God did?

The New Testament gives us insight on this issue. The name *Adam* is used in Scripture several times in different ways. One is a general representative term identifying mankind as a whole. The other is a specific reference to the man Adam. Paul says of Adam as a representative of humanity,

> Just as through one man sin entered into the world, and death through sin, and so death spread to all men, because all sinned—for until the Law sin was in the world, but sin is not imputed when there is no law. Nevertheless death reigned from Adam until Moses, even over those who had not sinned in the likeness of the offense of Adam, who is a type of Him who was to come. (Rom. 5:12–14)

But Paul draws another parallel between one man, Jesus, and one man, Adam: "For if by the transgression of the one, death reigned through the one, much more those who receive the abundance of grace and of the gift of righteousness will reign in life through the One, Jesus Christ" (Rom. 5:17). It is doubtful that Paul would have made such a pointed reference to sin entering the world through one man (Adam) if in fact that man had never existed. Further, in 1

Corinthians 15:21, Paul says that death came in by a man, and then in verse 22 he says, "For as in Adam all die, so also in Christ all will be made alive."

After reading these texts, our conclusion is obvious: it is next to impossible to believe that Paul didn't hold Adam to be a real human being who existed in the beginning of time as we know it.

What Was God's Image in Us to Look Like?

If we choose to believe in a literal Adam, then, we find that Adam's existence with Eve before the Fall gives us only one of two examples in the Bible of what mankind was intended to be in his original state. Mankind was created in the image of God, and before sin entered into his realm and life, he was unblemished and a perfect picture of humanity at its best. Our second example of humanity, created in the image of God and without blemish is, of course, Jesus.

In contrasting man as we know him today with these images of what mankind was intended to be, we can perceive the depth of depravity and corruption that sin has produced in the image of God in man. Paul tells us man was made in "the image and glory of God" (1 Cor. 11:7). But in what part of man did this image originally exist? Was it in our physical characteristics, our psychological makeup, our spiritual identity or a totality of all? What happened to the image of God in man at the Fall?

Jesus is the answer to these perplexing questions. He lived under divine revelation from His Father, so it can be deduced that we were once meant to do the same. So we can know that our consciousness—our mind, our understanding—was made in God's image. The image of God in us wasn't structural in the sense that mankind looked physically different after the Fall, but rather the Fall marred our internal relationship abilities that God had intended to function in man daily. This is why Jesus told us that the two greatest commandments were relational: we are to love God and love others (see Matt. 22:36–39).

Jesus had a perfect relationship with the Father. He knew His Father's heart, and He obeyed His Father's will. Jesus had a strong and compassionate love for others throughout His life and in His death on this earth. And it is here on Earth that God intends to restore His image in us as we love Him and love others.

The Image of God in Mankind Today

What are we to say as to the image of God in mankind today? Is there a remnant or vestige of His image left in the human race? The answer is yes. All mankind was created in God's image, every tongue, tribe and nation. Was that image imparted to our body, soul and spirit or just to our soul or our spirit? And what is left of it today?

The Old Testament indicates by the Hebrew word for *spirit* that man is a whole and that God's image in us permeated our entire being. The New Testament indicates that man is more than just a physical being—body and soul are also part of our makeup. But body and soul and spirit can be separated. Our body dies because of sin, but our spirit can live eternally and remain in God's image, so to speak. God's image also still remains at some level in the human soul, functioning as our conscience. This vestige of the image of God in us sets man apart from animals in that we are morally responsible.

Why is this question important if mankind is simply physical or of a dual nature (in which the body and mind are considered completely separate)? If mankind is treated as a compartmentalized being, then his spiritual condition could, theoretically, be separated from his physical person. Yet James warns against this. He tells us that the whole gospel is for the whole man. James 2:15–16 says, "If a brother or sister is without clothing and in need of daily food, and one of you says to them, 'Go in peace, be warmed and be filled,' and yet you do not give them what is necessary for their body, what use is that?"

Thus, we see that redemption is intended to permeate all humanity's being: our minds, our souls, our spirits and our physical person. Redemption restores God's image in us—the image that He first intended mankind to be characterized by prior to the Fall: the image of wholeness that causes us to value others in like manner, to live daily in purpose and destiny and to glorify God and reflect His image in mankind as He intended it to be.

8

Evil and Sin

The issues of evil and sin are two of the most difficult to deal with in the Bible, due to their direct impact on people's view of God and the extreme negativity that surrounds both issues.

Evil presents its own set of problems, before we even mention sin. It comes in several shapes and types. There is moral evil, which is fairly easy to explain, since it can be and often is a direct result of man's sin nature. But what is one to do with natural evil or disasters that kill and maim thousands?

It must be stated on the front end of any discussion on this topic that the issue of evil cannot be fully explained. People have made numerous attempts to do so and have formulated theories to lesson the tension, but none have fully answered the problem of evil in the world.

Why Does a Good God Allow Evil in the World?

Once we state that God is great and good but that evil resides in His creation, we have a dilemma that is not fully resolvable this side of heaven. Evil is, frankly, beyond human ability to deal with. It is by its very definition the most difficult issue for a person who believes in a thoughtful and personal God to resolve. Evil is the most severe of the intellectual problems facing the lover of a good God.

One fact that helps us deal with the issue is that man has a free will, and in order for us to be able to exercise that will, we must be able to do and to say things that go against the will of God. If God created a world with real moral choices, then we need to have warning signs when we are entering into sin and danger—which often come in the form of things that seem harmful and apparently unloving. But painful warnings ultimately produce restoration of life to those who retreat from the danger. This reminds us of the discipline of God that the writer of Hebrews describes: "All discipline for the moment seems not to be joyful, but sorrowful; yet to those who have been trained by it, afterwards it yields the peaceful fruit of righteousness" (Heb. 12:11).

One may question whether or not God is troubled by sin if He allows for it in His creation. But the account in Genesis 6–7 in which God wiped out all but Noah and his family because of the evil in people's hearts and lives should leave no doubt in our minds about God's feelings concerning immorality and the evil it wreaks upon humanity.

We also must remember that God has promised to work even within evil to bring about good: "And we know that God causes all things to work together for good to those who love God, to those who are called according to His purpose" (Rom. 8:28). As painful as it might be, it is important for us to note that God will use hardship and evil to build good if we trust Him. Second, we should consider the fact that although the dimension or duration of pain and evil are disturbing, if they bring about eternal life, they become an instrument of life.

Paul noted such a thing when he said, "I consider that the sufferings of this present time are not worthy to be compared with the glory that is to be revealed to us" (Rom. 8:18). Further he stated, "For this light momentary affliction is preparing for us an eternal weight of glory beyond all comparison" (2 Cor. 4:17, ESV). Sometimes evil is not as evil as it may seem, if it brings about a greater good. The rain that spoils one person's picnic may water hundreds of acres of farms that produce thousands of pounds of food to feed starving people in another part of the world. Is the rain bad or good?

The reality regarding evil is that most of it comes from what is known theologically as racial sin. This is not the prejudice of one race against another but the reality that because Adam's sin has permeated the entire human race, now all people sin. Without the first Fall, there would have been no death, and humankind would never have experienced the evil that death brings. Genesis 2:16–17 states, "The LORD God commanded the man, saying, 'From any tree of the garden you may eat freely; but from the tree of the knowledge of good and evil you shall not eat, for in the day that you eat from it you will surely die.'" And die we have done since that first sin took place.

Romans 8:20–22 further explains that much of natural evil is the result of this same sinfulness:

> For the creation was subjected to futility, not willingly, but because of Him who subjected it, in hope that the creation itself also will be set free from its slavery to corruption into the freedom of the glory of the children of God. For we know that the whole creation groans and suffers the pains of childbirth together until now.

But we are still faced with the irresolvable problem of God having declared His creation "very good" (Gen. 1:31) yet having to deal with this same creation's willingness to rebel against Him and to invite the evil of sin upon itself. The only answer to this problem is that for man to actually be free, really free, we had to have an option to exercise our free will outside the desires of God. Evil is that option. So God did not create sin, but He provided the option for us to sin—and the results that would accompany that choice.

Cause and Effect: Sin and Destruction

Dealing with the result of Adam and Eve's decision to exercise their free will brings us to the issue of sin and to the difficult question of why. Why disease, why misfortune, why ravaging disasters? Couldn't there have been a better way? Paul tells us that we must realize how grievous sin is to God: "Do not be deceived, God is not mocked; for whatever a man sows, this he will also reap. For the one who sows to his own flesh will from the flesh reap corruption, but the one who sows to the Spirit will from the Spirit reap eternal life" (Gal. 6:7–8).

The cause-and-effect relationships that God set into motion at creation—Paul calls this sowing and reaping—are numerous and often devastating. If one commits adultery and breaks the Law of God as it is found in Exodus 20:14—"You shall not commit adultery"—that person may lose his or her family, or worse, contract AIDS or some other sexually transmitted disease. Yet even with God's admonition to us to walk with God, we still choose to walk away and to face the evil our actions bring.

Lest we think that God does not understand the magnitude of these cause-and-effect relationships, we must never forget that God was so grieved by sinful man, Genesis 6:6 tells us, that He was driven to place His Son in the midst of our fallen world and to allow evil to kill Jesus in order that He might restore life and healing to His creation.

Missing the Mark

When dealing with sin, we should understand that there are several different words used in Scripture to describe sin and several different types of sin that man commits. There are sins born out of weakness and sins born out of willfulness. There are sins of inattention and sins of wrong motivation. There are sins of unbelief and sins of rebellion. The word most often used in the New Testament for *sin* means "to miss the mark," or to miss the target. The emphasis on this word is more on the outcome than on the motivation that led to the outcome.

What is sin? If sin is "missing the mark," what mark are we talking about? And do we miss it with our outward actions, or is sin our inward thoughts and responses? The Old Testament seems to put the weight on the outward, but Jesus clearly instructed otherwise in Matthew 5:21–22 and 27–28:

> You have heard that the ancients were told, "You shall not commit murder" and "Whoever commits murder shall be liable to the court." But I say to you that everyone who is angry with his brother shall be guilty before the court. . . . You have heard that it was said, "You shall not commit adultery"; but I say to you that everyone who looks at a woman with lust for her has already committed adultery with her in his heart.

The truth is, sin is both inward *and* outward. Sin is any lack of conformity with God's law, whether it is an active choice or an unwitting passive one. Sin is the failure to let God be God, to allow His rule over our lives, whether inward or outward. Sin is choosing something other than what God wants for us.

Sources of Sin

What is the source of sin in man today? It is certainly not God, for James tells us in James 1:13, "Let no one say when he is tempted, 'I am being tempted by God'; for God cannot be tempted by evil, and He Himself does not tempt anyone." The Bible teaches that sin is the sole responsibility of man. James goes on to say, "But each one is tempted when he is carried away and enticed by his own lust. Then when lust has conceived, it gives birth to sin; and when sin is accomplished, it brings forth death" (1:14–15).

This temptation that allures mankind into sin has several points of origin. First, as James states, there is the lust of man's heart for things he shouldn't desire.

Second, there is the tempter, Satan, who plants seeds of destruction in the hearts of people. We see this in the Garden of Eden: "Now the serpent was more crafty than any beast of the field which the Lord God had made. And he said to the woman, 'Indeed, has God said, "You shall not eat from any tree of the garden"?'" (Gen. 3:1). And we see this with Jesus when He was fasting in the desert:

> Then Jesus was led up by the Spirit into the wilderness to be tempted by the devil. And after He had fasted forty days and forty nights, He then became hungry. And the tempter came and said to Him, "If You are the Son of God, command that these stones become bread." (Matt. 4:1–3)

Finally, there is the spirit of the world, the spirit that seduces mankind into sin, which Paul alludes to in 1 Corinthians 2:12: "Now we have received, not the spirit of the world, but the Spirit who is from God, so that we may know the things freely given to us by God."

Sin's Results and God's Provision

The results of sin are clear: "For the wages of sin is death, but the free gift of God is eternal life in Christ Jesus our Lord" (Rom. 6:23). But the wages of sin are also bondage to its control and to its power to blind and wound in this life as it steals from us the next life. Sin is totally permeating and deceitful. But the good news of Romans 6:23 remains ever true: the free gift of life and freedom is Jesus Christ, who alone sets man free from sin.

9

Christ and Salvation

The concept of salvation and the deep, impacting, life-changing work of Christ can and should be relevant to all people. There is an obvious gulf between hurting people and a life-giving, healing God that Jesus hungers to bridge. Some people who have given themselves to God speak of salvation as past tense—"I have been saved"—while others speak in future tense—"I will be saved." And there are those who view salvation as a process and who state, "I am being saved." Saved from or for what?

The biblical concept of salvation is rooted and grounded in the reality that sin separates and stands between God and man. Jesus said that He came to give life and give it to the fullest: "The thief comes only to steal and kill and destroy; I came that they may have life, and have it abundantly" (John 10:10). This is the heart of the salvation message: salvation is an impartation of life that can come only through the person of Jesus.

How does a person enter into salvation? Are the steps the same for everyone? I love to ask people if surrendering their will to God is part of getting saved. Nearly 100 percent of those in church answer yes. I then ask them how much of their will they need to surrender to get their names written in the Book of Life. They usually answer in unison, "One hundred percent," to which response I laugh and then ask, "If that is the case, why do you sin after you get saved? If 100 percent of your will was God's, you would never sin again."

See, friends, we do surrender our will in order to enter into the salvation Jesus offers. But how much of our will? I have no idea. Enough to get our name in the Book of Life. But the process of sanctification, the daily surrender to the Lord that each of us must maintain, clearly assures us that we didn't lay down every bit of our will at the altar of salvation.

Predestination versus Man's Free Will

To understand the process of salvation, we need to address the issue of predestination, which has historically created multiple problems for the church. Predestination refers to God choosing some individuals for eternal life and not others. The thought process regarding the doctrine of predestination goes like this: Since man has sinned, can he or does he even have the ability to seek after God? Is he now so marred in his spirit that any thought in his mind of a loving God is lost? If so, God must initiate salvation, because man cannot.

Let's unfold this thought. The doctrine of predestination is actually the outcome of another doctrine, that of the total depravity of man. This teaching states that once Adam sinned, all mankind was now marred—and in that sinful state we lost the ability to freely choose to live and to walk with God. So even though mankind has a free will, we cannot exercise that will for good. Thus, it is impossible for us to choose to be saved. Therefore, predestination states, none of us can or will be saved without God choosing us and ordaining us into eternity.

Augustine was the initial proponent of this type of predestination doctrine, but over the centuries many others have supported this position, including Thomas Aquinas and Martin Luther. John Calvin, however, is remembered more than any other for his work on predestination.

Calvin actually developed the election proposition (God choosing some for heaven) into what is known as double election: some are elected to heaven and some are elected to hell. He insisted that this type of predestination would not lead to excessive living, as many contended it would. But it stands to reason that if God elects some to heaven and others to hell, then those who are elected to heaven might live as if they're headed for hell, since they know that they'll ultimately get to heaven anyway. Obviously this view of the Christian life lacks the balance that the Bible demands.

Jacob Arminius took issue with Calvin's doctrine, contending that such a proposition as total election, or predestination, violated man's free will. Arminius contended that God has given sufficient grace to all to believe if they so choose, and God predestines those whom He knows will exercise that grace.

Calvinist Views

In a rebuttal to Arminius's views, Calvinists later developed Calvin's beliefs to include what is known as TULIP, which stands for five doctrinal points:

> Total depravity
> Unconditional predestination
> Limited atonement
> Irresistible grace
> Perseverance

Calvinists see the whole of the human race as so lost in sin that no one is able to respond at any point to the grace of God. They believe that since God is sovereign and free to do as He wills, He can choose one person over another for salvation without being capricious. Romans 9:20–21 seems to support this position:

> Who are you, O man, who answers back to God? The thing molded will not say to the molder, "Why did you make me like this," will it? Or does not the potter have a right over the clay, to make from the

same lump one vessel for honorable use and another for common use?

Further, other verses seem to support the proposition of election. Ephesians 1:4–5 is often offered as proof of this doctrine: "He chose us in Him before the foundation of the world, that we would be holy and blameless before Him. In love He predestined us to adoption as sons through Jesus Christ to Himself, according to the kind intention of His will." To those who believe in predestination, election is seen as a decision of the Father that expresses His good will to those He chooses to save. Election is not based on anyone's merit; it is the source of faith, not the result of it. Election is also efficacious, or certain in its effect, and it is unconditional and immutable, or absolute. It is not based on any action of man, and it cannot be reversed.

Arminian Views

The problem most people find here is the seeming inconsistency between election and the free will of man. Are we just puppets, or do we have a say in our destiny? Further, if salvation is all decided beforehand and people cannot freely choose to follow Christ, why should we witness to anyone or spend time on the mission field or serve others in the hope that they will open up to Jesus?

Arminianism, which follows the teaching of Arminius, contends that there is far too much control in the Calvinists' position. Where does human free will enter into the equation? What about all the verses in Scripture that indicate that people have a choice in the matter of salvation? Isaiah states, "Ho! Every one who thirsts, come to the waters; and you who have no money come, buy and eat" (55:1). And Jesus said in Matthew 11:28, "Come to Me, all who are weary and heavy-laden, and I will give you rest." These and other verses seem to make it clear that anyone who comes to the Lord will be saved.

Arminians believe that all people have sufficient grace to believe and to be saved. They agree with Calvinists that mankind is depraved, but they believe that God offers grace freely to all. In other words, He offers what is called prevenient grace, a grace that draws people to Christ and helps them overcome obstacles they may face in regard to salvation. Without this grace life is fatalistic, Arminians argue. If God has everyone's salvation or damnation determined, they question, why would anyone strive to do right?

Reconciling God's Sovereign Choice and Man's Free Will

How do we reconcile these two views? First, the Bible speaks at length about the deep level of human depravity. Paul is especially clear about this when he contends in Romans 3 that things are terribly dark for the human race. He states,

> "There is none righteous, not even one; there is none who understands, there is none who seeks for God; all have turned aside, together they have become useless; there is none who does good, there is not even one." "Their throat is an open grave, with their tongues they keep deceiving," "the poison of asps is under their lips," "whose mouth is full of cursing and bitterness; their feet are swift to shed blood, destruction and misery are in their paths, and the path of peace they have not known." "There is no fear of God before their eyes." (3:10–18)

This is a very definite statement, and we can rest assured that Paul wouldn't have chosen these words if they did not say exactly what he intended to convey.

This dire state of mankind, however, leaves us little room to argue for anything less than the Arminians' call for prevenient grace—a grace that nullifies the numbing, blinding result of sin in people's lives and draws them to Christ, enabling them to make a decision for God. Jesus Himself declared, "For God so loved the world, that He gave His only begotten Son, that whoever believes in Him shall not perish, but have eternal life" (John 3:16). Why would Jesus have made such a statement that includes the word "whoever" if God had predetermined that some would come and others would not, thus nullifying any chance of man exercising his free will? Such a view makes no sense whatsoever.

So there is no question about the depravity of man, and there is no question that God's prevenient grace overcomes our depravity and draws us to Christ. But it is also true that there is not a lot of room for us to argue against predestination, since Scripture clearly states that God "predestined us to adoption as sons" (Eph. 1:5).

What does all this mean?

There are two crucial roles played in our salvation experience: God's role in wooing and drawing us to Himself and our role in exercising our will to respond to God's beckoning call.

Simply stated, Jesus' shed blood made a way for our salvation, according to Hebrews 9:22: "According to the Law, one may almost say, all things are cleansed with blood, and without shedding of blood there is no forgiveness." Jesus shed His blood for our forgiveness, and through His sacrifice God has made a way to heal, redeem, restore and renew mankind—and His way is in the person of Jesus. Jesus is God's salvation message, the bridge between heaven and Earth, and He holds a wooing grace that allows all of us, no matter how wicked and twisted we are, to hear the heart of God the Father and His love for us.

Then, since God has made a way for us, our will comes directly into play in the salvation experience. Now we must decide whether or not we will receive God's gift of salvation. So we can say that the door to heaven is open to all, as John 3:16 tells us: "whoever" wants to may enter. But, once we walk through that door, the sign on the back of the door will read, "You were chosen before the beginning of time."

These two tracks run side by side simultaneously throughout Scripture—the sovereignty of God and the free will of man.

With this in mind, we can say with confidence that God is just and loving, that He desires none to perish and that we must evangelize, because we have no idea who is and who is not being called by God and who will and who will not respond to His Spirit's call.

When a person is called, an unfolding of faith must occur within him for salvation to be complete. The call of God, though, is crucial to salvation. How does this call come, and is it only open to certain people? According to Jesus in Matthew 11:28, the entire world receives a general call: "Come to Me, all who are weary and heavy-laden, and I will give you rest." The words "all who are weary" basically opens the door to all.

In many texts, however, the New Testament implies that there is a further, more specific call. Romans 8:30 says, "And these whom He predestined, He also called; and these whom He called, He also justified; and these whom He justified, He also glorified." So only those whom God specifically calls with this special calling will be saved. Reference to this particular call is found in many other texts, including Luke 14:23, Romans 1:7, 1 Corinthians 1:9, Ephesians 1:18 and Philippians 3:14.

We would refer to this special calling as the Holy Spirit's conviction, or His moving on a person. Arminians, as we have seen, refer to this as prevenient grace, and it logically comes before conversion. Then salvation is dependent upon a person responding to this call. When a person surrenders his will to this call of God, that individual enters into what Jesus called new birth, or new life. We see this illustrated in Acts 16:31: "Believe in the Lord Jesus, and you will be saved, you and your household."

So a response of faith to God's call, which then manifests repentance, will initiate a person's conversion experience—and this then leads to regeneration of the individual. But without repentance there can be no salvation, for the Scripture declares in Acts 2:38, "Repent, and each of you be baptized in the name of Jesus Christ for the forgiveness of your sins; and you will receive the gift of the Holy Spirit."

Salvation takes place when God visits a person with a special revelatory call and the person chooses to respond with both repentance and faith to the person of Jesus. This leads to conversion of the individual. This person is moved from death to life, leading further to his or her regeneration, or being born again, as Jesus described it in John 3:7.

10

The Atonement

It should be stated at the outset that this doctrine of the atonement of Christ is the fundamental doctrine of the Bible. It is the foundation for all other doctrines, and it is highly impacted by each of the other major doctrines.

Before we move into our discussion of the atonement, it should be noted that Christ came to fulfill three distinct roles: prophet, priest and king. These roles, or offices, help us to understand Jesus' functions while He was here on Earth.

As prophet, Jesus came to fulfill and to reveal the heart of God. Jesus said of Himself, "A prophet is not without honor except in his hometown and in his own household" (Matt. 13:57). He was sent from God, and like other prophets, He brought the word of the Lord—and He *was* the Word of the Lord. He proclaimed judgment and salvation.

As king, Jesus brought the dominion of God into the hearts of men. He ruled over nature as well (see Col. 1:17), and as Isaiah 9:7 proclaims, "There will be no end to the increase of His government."

As priest, Jesus came to reconcile the world to God. He came, as it were, to mediate between God and man. He is, as John 17 declares, an intercessor on our behalf. This role of Jesus as priest is the crux of the doctrine of atonement. Jesus came to save the lost and to heal the breach that sin had brought about between God and man.

When Jesus came, it was in humiliation. He was born poor, in a stable, and He was bound by the frailty of humanity. As John 1:14 states, "the Word became flesh." Jesus gave up His rightful place, Philippians 2:7 tells us, to take on "the form of a bond-servant." He gave up His right to exercise His divine attributes and submitted Himself to become the Lamb of God. This led to His ultimate humiliation and death, but it also led to His great exaltation: the resurrection from the dead. This magnificent triumph inflicted a mortal blow to the power of sin over mankind and opened the door to a new dimension of relationship between God and man. Yet Christ's greatest exaltation still awaits, as it is bound up in His return to Earth to set right all that has been broken by sin and to defeat all death.

Various Views on the Atonement

As our priest, Jesus came to heal our relationship with God. This is known as the atonement. How this actually unfolds is a point of much debate and disagreement. There are essentially five primary doctrines pertaining to the theory of atonement.

The first is known as the Socinian theory, named after Faustus and Laelius Socinus. Basically, this theory states that humans are capable of following God's will by emulating Christ's example. They also believe that God is not a God of retribution but rather is benevolent regarding sin. Followers of this theory believe that Christ's death was not supernatural but rather a perfect illustration for all to see of God's total love for mankind—a picture that was meant to inspire us to love others as God loves us. The Socinian theory basically states that Jesus is our example to follow rather than our atoning sacrifice.

Second is the theory of moral influence, which says that Jesus' death helped to rectify man's fear of God's judgment by showing us how much God loves us. The major effect of Christ's death was on man recognizing God's kindness, not on God being satisfied with Jesus' sacrifice for sin. This theory minimizes God's qualities of justice, holiness and righteousness and instead maximizes His love and emphasizes His empathy. There is nothing in man's nature that is fundamentally wrong, this theory says, that a little love from God won't fix. All man needs to see is that God loved him so much that He was willing to die for him.

The third major theory is the governmental theory, whose name indicates that it deals primarily with the seriousness of sin and its violation of the law. God loves mankind, who has violated God's law and needs to pay for his sin. But in the governmental theory of atonement, God's laws must be satisfied more than God's just nature. According to this view Christ was punished so that God could forgive sin while at the same time keeping humanity from dealing with sin's adverse effects themselves. Jesus' punishment also enabled people to understand how bad sin is. Unfortunately, there is no real scriptural basis for this theory; it is built entirely upon scriptural inferences.

The ransom theory is the fourth major theory of the atonement. Basically, it states Christ's declaration in Matthew 20:28 that Jesus came "to give His life a ransom for many." What it doesn't explain is whom it is that Jesus paid this ransom to: is it Satan, or is it God the Father? Most of those holding to this theory speculate that the ransom was paid to Satan, and he was quick to receive it when he realized that Jesus was willing to trade Himself for those trapped in sin and bondage to the devil. Fortunately, Satan's blind greediness caused him to miss the reality that Jesus could and would survive even death and therefore conquer Satan's schemes over mankind. In this view Christ's atoning work was not directed toward man but to another, Satan.

Finally, the last theory is the satisfaction theory. According to this premise, Christ died to satisfy the nature of a God who was demanding and, in the eyes of some, retributive. Not surprisingly, this theory arose during a period that was highly influenced by the Roman Catholic Church's emphasis on a penitential system of release from sin. This system held that one could avoid paying for his sins eternally if he made payment for it in this life, or paid penance. This payment for sins committed often came in the form of money. The crux of this theory is that since man's sin separated him from God and thus death entered into all humankind, in order to save some, God sent His Son to make penance, so to speak, for our sin.

Jesus: The Sacrifice and Substitute for Our Sin

Each of these five theories holds some point of truth, although none of them combines the fullness of the atonement with all that it was meant to accomplish. In order to fully explain the atonement, one must examine several issues.

First, *the nature of God*. God is loving, but He is also holy and just. God gave the law not to trap mankind but to reveal a part of His character and person to us. Disobeying the law is serious not just because it is the law of God but because it is an attack on the person of God and on His holiness. Therefore, violating the law ends in death. It did for Adam, and it does for us.

With this view of God in place, we next need a biblical perspective of *the nature of man*. Man is, as we know, fallen. Once sin entered into our lives, we became totally incapable of freeing ourselves from its bondage. So it is that we became totally depraved.

Third, we need to understand *the nature of Christ*. The nature of Jesus Christ is essential to our salvation. Jesus is both God and man, and it must be so in order for His death to atone for the sins of all mankind. Galatians 4:4–5 states, "When the fullness of the time came, God sent forth His Son, born of a woman, born under the Law, so that He might redeem those who were under the Law, that we might receive the adoption as sons." Jesus was, as we are, "born under the Law."

Because of who He is, Jesus was able to extricate us from the law's demands by giving Himself as the sacrificial payment that the Old Testament law required (see Lev. 1:3–4). Isaiah 53:6–7 clearly proclaims this, declaring,

All of us like sheep have gone astray, each of us has turned to his own way; but the LORD has caused the iniquity of us all to fall on Him. He was oppressed and He was afflicted, yet He did not open His mouth; like a lamb that is led to slaughter, and like a sheep that is silent before its shearers, so He did not open His mouth.

In the New Testament we see Jesus proclaim Himself as a ransom (see Matt. 20:28), a substitute (see John 15:13) and most often, as we are about to see, a sacrifice. John the Baptist said of Jesus as he introduced Him to an Old Testament crowd, "Behold, the Lamb of God, who takes away the sin of the world!" (John 1:29). Caiaphas said the same: "You know nothing at all, nor do you take into account that it is expedient for you that one man die for the people, and that the whole nation not perish" (John 11:49–50). We find Paul making similar statements throughout his writings, for example, in 2 Corinthians 5:19 he said, "God was in Christ reconciling the world to Himself, not counting their trespasses against them," and in Romans 5:8, "God shows his love for us in that while we were still sinners, Christ died for us" (ESV).

Paul also clearly regarded the death of Christ as propitiatory, that is, it took away God's wrath toward mankind. We see this in Romans 1:18: "The wrath of God is revealed from heaven against all ungodliness and unrighteousness of men who suppress the truth in unrighteousness," and again in 2:5–6: "Because of your stubbornness and unrepentant heart you are storing up wrath for yourself in the day of wrath and revelation of the righteous judgment of God, who will render to each person according to his deeds."

So we see that the atonement consists of Jesus being a sacrifice for our sin, a substitution—His death in place of ours—and a means of reconciliation, as it ended our hostility with God and removed the estrangement between Him and us. Each of these aspects of the atonement is carefully addressed in the theory known as the penal-substitution theory. This theory confirms that humanity is depraved and totally unable to meet our obligation as far as it concerns the sin in our life.

The penal-substitution theory also makes it clear that God's nature isn't just to love man and forgive him for his sin, nor, on the other hand, is it simply to be angry at sin, but it states that God is both righteous and loving. As John 3:16 declares, "God so loved the world, that He gave His only begotten Son"—and He gave Him in order to fulfill our debt and to remove His just anger from us. This can only happen by grace; there is no room for man's hand in our own salvation. Accordingly, this salvation is accomplished by the death of Christ and by that means alone.

11
The Assurance of Salvation

Like most of the theological arguments surrounding salvation (the discussion of soteriology), Calvinists and Arminians drive the discussion. This is the case with the issue of the assurance of the believer as well. Can one who has been saved by Jesus lose his or her salvation? Can one who is saved rest in his or her salvation, or must the person do something to secure its permanence?

Arminians and Calvinists believe that God is both willing and able to keep His promises. Both believe that the Holy Spirit is at work in all believers. Both believe that true salvation is complete and provided by God alone. However, that is where they quit agreeing and begin to sharply diverge.

Is Our Salvation Secure—or Can We Lose It?

Calvinists believe that God has elected some to salvation and not others. If a person is elected, then, it reasons, that person will be saved and permanently so, for none can thwart the will of God. This position can be defended biblically by texts that seem to be in conclusive support of it. First Peter 1:3–5 is one such passage:

> Blessed be the God and Father of our Lord Jesus Christ, who according to His great mercy has caused us to be born again to a living hope through the res-

urrection of Jesus Christ from the dead, to obtain an inheritance which is imperishable and undefiled and will not fade away, reserved in heaven for you, who are protected by the power of God through faith for a salvation ready to be revealed in the last time.

Here we are told that our inheritance will be "imperishable," "undefiled," and protected. This text does not stand alone in such bold affirmations. Romans 8:38–39 concurs, stating that it would be impossible to separate a person from so great a salvation:

I am convinced that neither death, nor life, nor angels, nor principalities, nor things present, nor things to come, nor powers, nor height, nor depth, nor any other created thing, will be able to separate us from the love of God, which is in Christ Jesus our Lord.

Moreover, the greatest promise regarding the permanence of salvation comes from Jesus Himself, who said,

My sheep hear My voice, and I know them, and they follow Me; and I give eternal life to them, and they will never perish; and no one will snatch them out of My hand. My Father, who has given them to Me, is greater than all; and no one is able to snatch them out of the Father's hand. I and the Father are one. (John 10:27–30)

Obviously, this passage leaves no room to believe that a person's salvation could be stolen by the enemy; in fact, it actually states that those who are saved "will never perish." This is certainly the strongest argument one could hope for in the debate over the permanence of salvation.

But however difficult it seems after reading these verses to believe that a person could lose his salvation, there is a strong opinion in favor of this view. The Arminian's position is built on several texts that seem to leave the door open to a person losing his or her salvation. For instance, Jesus stated,

> See to it that no one misleads you. For many will come in My name, saying, "I am the Christ," and will mislead many.... Many false prophets will arise and will mislead many. Because lawlessness is increased, most people's love will grow cold. But the one who endures to the end, he will be saved. (Matt. 24:4–5, 11–13)

Why would Jesus have said "the one who endures to the end will be saved" if absolute certainty of salvation was a foregone conclusion—if it were not possible for those who are saved to be misled and to fall away? Colossians 1:21–23 seems to confirm such thinking:

> Although you were formerly alienated and hostile in mind, engaged in evil deeds, yet He has now reconciled you in His fleshly body through death, in order to present you before Him holy and blameless and beyond reproach—if indeed you continue in the faith firmly established and steadfast, and not moved away from the hope of the gospel that you have heard, which was proclaimed in all creation under heaven, and of which I, Paul, was made a minister.

Paul's choice of words seems to imply a contingency. He states that those who were once hostile to God are now reconciled to Him and set for eternal life *if* they continue in the faith. But what if they don't? What if they stumble and walk away from Christ? Will they lose their salvation? Arminians would argue yes:

> In the case of those who have once been enlightened and have tasted of the heavenly gift and have been made partakers of the Holy Spirit, and have tasted the good word of God and the powers of the age to come, and then have fallen away, it is impossible to renew them again to repentance, since they again crucify to themselves the Son of God and put Him to open shame. (Heb. 6:4–6)

Arminians also point out that people must have the ability to fall, or to opt out of salvation, if they are to retain their own free will. If it is certain that we cannot lose our salvation, then, they reason, we have lost the choice of apostasy. If that is the case, we also lose our free will, and thus they argue correctly that Scripture exhorts people to exercise our free will and to choose God but that in order to do so our will must remain free.

Surrendered to Salvation

How are these two positions to be reconciled? First, Jesus seemed to reject outright the possibility of true believers losing their salvation when He stated, "They will never perish" (John 10:28). The question then arises: did the author of Hebrews mean that those who fall away were never really saved?

Hebrews 6:4 states that these people were once partakers of the Holy Spirit. And Romans 8:9 tells us that if a person has the Holy Spirit, then he is saved: "You are not in the flesh but in the Spirit, if indeed the Spirit of God dwells in you. But if anyone does not have the Spirit of Christ, he does not belong to Him." So it appears that those who fell away from Christ in the book of Hebrews, since they partook of the Holy Spirit, must have been authentic believers.

The Calvinist would argue that people do have free will to fall away but that the writer of Hebrews was offering a hypothetical possibility of a person falling out of the faith, knowing that the person would never choose to do so if he were elected and sealed into salvation. But can a person choose to leave the faith on his own volition? It took the person's will, remember, to surrender to God and be saved in the first place. Jesus said in John 10:27, "No one will snatch them out of My hand," but does that preclude a believer from removing himself?

Jesus made it clear that not everyone who calls on the name of the Lord is truly His. In Matthew 7:15–16 He declared that people would be known by their fruits, not their words: "Beware of the false prophets, who come to you in sheep's clothing, but inwardly are ravenous wolves. You will know them by their fruits." Further on in the same text Jesus proclaimed that there will be many who will call on Him and invoke His name in ministry and even do miracles in His name yet not be saved:

> Not everyone who says to Me, "Lord, Lord," will enter the kingdom of heaven, but he who does the will of My Father who is in heaven will enter. Many will say to Me on that day, "Lord, Lord, did we not prophesy in Your name, and in Your name cast out demons, and in Your name perform many miracles?" And then I will declare to them, "I never knew you; depart from Me, you who practice lawlessness." (7:21–23)

This same theme runs through the parable of the sower, which indicates that there will be people who appear to be Christians, people who will begin to respond to the call of the Spirit but who will never surrender enough to enter into the fullness of salvation. Matthew 13:23 says that only those who bear fruit are really saved: "And the one on whom seed was sown on the good soil, this is the man who hears the word and understands it; who indeed bears fruit and brings forth, some a hundredfold, some sixty, and some thirty."

In summation, it should be stated that there is no doctrine of insecurity found in the Bible. Once we are surrendered to salvation and sealed by the Spirit into salvation (see Eph. 1:13), we can rest in assurance that even if we stumble, we will never fall out of the grace of God. It is clear, when we look at the whole counsel of Scripture, that some believers will backslide—including the apostle Peter, who, in his weakness, turned away from the Lord and denied Him—yet never lose their salvation. In fact, God used Peter's situation to strengthen his faith and his ability to lead others with the heart of God. Always remember that it is as Jesus has spoken: His sheep will "never perish" (John 10:28).

12

Justification

Justification is the instantaneous restoration of righteousness that God gives to those who open their hearts and lives to His forgiveness. Justification is judicial in nature, meaning that it pertains to the law of God and the standing of the individual believer in relationship to that law.

At the Fall sin entered into the human race and forever blemished mankind. Human nature was corrupted, and mankind failed to fulfill the expectation of God and His law. Man was now found to be in unrighteous standing before God. The guilt that hung over all mankind was due to the Fall and to the curse that entered into humanity. Justification is the lifting of that curse and therefore of our guiltiness.

Guilt Abolished Once for All

Under the curse of the Fall, God came to be seen as the judge of His creation and not the Father of it. Only those who have been acquitted of the guilt of the Fall experience the full meaning of having God as their Father once again. This restoration can only take place upon the receiving of Jesus' blood atonement by faith as a payment for one's unrighteousness and guilt.

Romans 4:3–5 describes this impartation of righteousness by faith:

> What does the Scripture say? "Abraham believed God, and it was credited to him as righteousness." Now to the one who works, his wage is not credited as a favor, but as what is due. But to the one who does not work, but believes in Him who justifies the ungodly, his faith is credited as righteousness.

When we believe in the atoning work of the cross and accept it as our own, we are immediately put in right standing with our heavenly Father, and we no longer face the condemnation we deserve for breaking the law of God. Romans 8:32–34 describes this:

> He who did not spare His own Son, but delivered Him over for us all, how will He not also with Him freely give us all things? Who will bring a charge against God's elect? God is the one who justifies; who is the one who condemns? Christ Jesus is He who died, yes, rather who was raised, who is at the right hand of God, who also intercedes for us.

This act of justification is not the same as the process of sanctification, which is the daily outworking of our forgiveness. Justification declares once for all that the guilt of our sin is abolished—it is not a matter of infusing a believer with holiness on a daily basis. The aspect of maturing in faith over time is the work of sanctification. Justification is the reality that God no longer sees the believer standing on his or her own merit but on the work of the cross.

Christ died to fulfill the payment due for sin, as Romans 3:23–24 declares: "For all have sinned and fall short of the glory of God, being justified as a gift by His grace through the redemption which is in Christ Jesus." It is at the cross of Christ that believers are set free from the requirement of the law, which demands a payment of death for sin: "For the wages of sin is death, but the free gift of God is eternal life in Christ Jesus our Lord" (Rom. 6:23). Thus, justification is a gift, a free gift, that cannot be entered into on human merit. No amount of work can satisfy the demands of the law.

Justification Is Not Earned

Because justification is a gift, many struggle with receiving it freely. There is in most of humankind an ingrained sense that we need to earn a position of favor with God. Some point to the Old Testament as an example of people who worked their way into righteousness with God, but clearly that is mistaken thinking. Galatians 3:6–9 states what the Bible delivers as obvious—that Abraham, the father of our faith, *believed* God, just as we are to believe God, and that by his faith he was established and justified before God:

> Even so Abraham believed God, and it was reckoned to him as righteousness. Therefore, be sure that it is those who are of faith who are sons of Abraham. The Scripture, foreseeing that God would justify the Gentiles by faith, preached the gospel beforehand to Abraham, saying, "All the nations will be blessed in you." So then those who are of faith are blessed with Abraham, the believer.

Attempting to work our way to God is the source of much frustration in the church and in the world. The Scripture is clear about the fact that justification is an act of faith and not of works. Those who rely on works actually find themselves under the curse of the law, according to Paul:

> As many as are of the works of the Law are under a curse; for it is written, "Cursed is everyone who

does not abide by all things written in the book of the law, to perform them." Now that no one is justified by the Law before God is evident; for, "The righteous man shall live by faith." (Gal. 3:10–11)

The only way out from under this curse is to trust by faith that Christ's death satisfied the law and now covers the sin of those who trust in Him: "Christ redeemed us from the curse of the Law, having become a curse for us—for it is written, 'Cursed is everyone who hangs on a tree'" (Gal. 3:13).

So forgiveness of sins and the justification that comes with it are received by faith alone. However, that doesn't preclude the believer from serving and working for Christ once he has entered into this life of faith. Ephesians 2:8–10 is clear about this fact:

> For by grace you have been saved through faith; and that not of yourselves, it is the gift of God; not as a result of works, so that no one may boast. For we are His workmanship, created in Christ Jesus for good works, which God prepared beforehand so that we would walk in them.

We are saved by grace and then we are established into Christ as His *poema*, or workmanship. This indicates that we are first to believe and establish a life-giving relationship with Jesus, and then out of that relationship, we will love and serve the Lord by doing "good works, which God prepared beforehand so that we would walk in them." So the eternal consequences of sin are atoned for by Jesus at the cross.

A New Creation in Christ

What remains, however, is the reality that the consequences of sin may still impact our day-to-day living. The fact that Jesus died for us on the cross doesn't diminish the truth that the death that entered the world at the Fall will still overtake our physical bodies before we experience the fullness of eternal life. Or if someone who has chosen to live for Christ stumbles and sins in a fashion that wounds or impacts another, it doesn't mean that the believer will not suffer the consequences for his or her actions in this life.

Does this mean that the forgiveness promised by God through Christ isn't real or that it isn't sufficient to cover and restore one's life completely? The answer is a resounding no. Christ's payment at the cross fully satisfies the requirement of God, and it completely justifies those who receive it. However, the Bible also teaches that we will reap what we sow: "Do not be deceived, God is not mocked; for whatever a man sows, this he will also reap. For the one who sows to his own flesh will from the flesh reap corruption, but the one who sows to the Spirit will from the Spirit reap eternal life" (Gal. 6:7–8).

So justification impacts our eternal standing with God, cleansing us from all unrighteousness in His sight. God now sees us "in Christ," without blemish or sin but as a new creation: "If anyone is in Christ, he is a new creature; the old things passed away; behold, new things have come" (2 Cor. 5:17). Furthermore, we find that Christ is also in us: "To [the saints] God willed to make known what is the riches of the glory of this mystery among the Gentiles, which is Christ in you, the hope of glory" (Col. 1:27). We are no longer on our own before God—we are in Christ, and He is in us. God now views us as He views His own Son: complete and righteous.

13

Regeneration/Sanctification

The Christian life was never meant to be static. God intended it to be ever flowing and changing. It was always intended to be a process of growth and maturity empowered by the Holy Spirit in the hearts of those who surrender to Him. When discussing the process of regeneration, or sanctification, it is crucial to note at the beginning that it is just that—a process. Unlike justification, which is an instantaneous event in which we are made right before the Father through union with Christ and washing by His blood, sanctification is an ongoing daily process of dying to one's desires and hungers in order that one may live for God.

Desiring Righteousness out of Love for Christ

This ongoing work of regeneration, also known as sanctification, can only take place as a person's relationship with Jesus grows and matures, for it is God's Spirit that indwells and empowers the new life of the believer. Jesus referred to this in John 15:4–7 when He discussed our need to abide in Him:

> Abide in Me, and I in you. As the branch cannot bear fruit of itself unless it abides in the vine, so neither can you unless you abide in Me. I am the vine, you are the branches; he who abides in Me and I in him, he bears much fruit, for apart from Me you

can do nothing. If anyone does not abide in Me, he is thrown away as a branch and dries up; and they gather them, and cast them into the fire and they are burned. If you abide in Me, and My words abide in you, ask whatever you wish, and it will be done for you.

In Philippians 3:7–11, Paul also spoke of our need to pursue a deep relationship with Christ, no matter the cost:

> Whatever things were gain to me, those things I have counted as loss for the sake of Christ. More than that, I count all things to be loss in view of the surpassing value of knowing Christ Jesus my Lord, for whom I have suffered the loss of all things, and count them but rubbish so that I may gain Christ, and may be found in Him, not having a righteousness of my own derived from the Law, but that which is through faith in Christ, the righteousness which comes from God on the basis of faith, that I may know Him and the power of His resurrection and the fellowship of His sufferings, being conformed to His death; in order that I may attain to the resurrection from the dead.

For Paul, the outcome of this pursuit of Christ was clear: he would receive the righteousness of God, and not by works but by being in intimate relationship with God by faith. The cost would be real—Paul would have to give up some things in order to get other things from God. He might have to suffer during this life, but that suffering would certainly pale in comparison to the reward he would receive in the next life. This choice for Paul wasn't born out of a desire to keep the law or simply to please God. This desire was born out of the deep love and friendship he had developed in Christ. Jesus had promised that such a relationship was possible:

> Greater love has no one than this, that one lay down his life for his friends. You are My friends if you do what I command you. No longer do I call you slaves, for the slave does not know what his master is doing; but I have called you friends, for all things that I have heard from My Father I have made known to you. (John 15:13–15)

Thus, Paul was no longer under compulsion to keep the Law of Moses; he was now free to serve Jesus in his new life in Christ out of a love relationship.

The Purpose of the Law

"So," one might ask, "what role does the law play then in a believer's life in respect to his spiritual maturity and growth?"

First of all, we need to understand that the Law of Moses never saved anyone. Some have said, "There are two ways to be saved: keep all the laws, or give yourself to Jesus." This is biblically incorrect, for the Bible never says that the law was given in order to save people. Scripture is very clear about the fact that there is only one way into eternity: Jesus.

But second, though the law doesn't save us, it does have a purpose: the law is a plumb line, a measuring stick, so that people can know how they stand in relationship to the perfection of God. When we see how imperfect we are, we are driven to Jesus for the salvation that He and He alone holds for us. The book of Romans articulates this in several places: Romans 3:20 says, "By the works of the Law no flesh will be justified in His sight; for through the Law comes the knowledge of sin." Romans 5:13 speaks of the need for the law to define sin for us: "For until the Law sin was in the world, but sin is not imputed when there is no law." Romans 5:20 further states that the law would not only help us to see our sin, but it would, in fact, cause our sin nature to react in further defiance of God, revealing an even deeper need in us for God's grace: "The Law came in so that the transgression would increase; but where sin increased, grace abounded all the more."

So it is only by attaching ourselves to the heart of Christ that we can mature in faith. Spiritual growth is accomplished in us by the work of the Holy Spirit, whose role it is to empower, heal and renew the believer in Christ's image. Romans 8:3–4 describes this journey as one that fulfills the requirements of the law:

> For what the Law could not do, weak as it was through the flesh, God did: sending His own Son in the likeness of sinful flesh and as an offering for sin, He condemned sin in the flesh, so that the requirement of the Law might be fulfilled in us, who do not walk according to the flesh but according to the Spirit.

Partnering with the Holy Spirit

This does not mean that those who love Christ and are called into His grace are not also bound to respond to Him and His commandments. In John 14:15 Jesus said that if we don't obey His commandments, we probably don't love Him: "If you love Me, you will keep My commandments." So we find a great tension here. On one hand, we are free from the law because we are saved by grace, yet on the other hand, we are bound to obey the commands of Christ. Paul spoke to this tension in the book of Galatians, when he asked a penetrating question of those who felt that they had to mature and grow in their own salvation:

> You foolish Galatians, who has bewitched you, before whose eyes Jesus Christ was publicly portrayed as crucified? This is the only thing I want to find out from you: did you receive the Spirit by the works of the Law, or by hearing with faith? Are you so foolish? Having begun by the Spirit, are you now being perfected by the flesh? Did you suffer so many things in vain—if indeed it was in vain? So then, does He who provides you with the Spirit and works miracles among you, do it by the works of the Law, or by hearing with faith? (3:1–5)

Paul asks, "If you began your relationship with Jesus by the ministry of the Holy Spirit, how do you think it should continue if it is to grow and mature: by working it out in your own power or by surrendering and partnering with the Holy Spirit's work in you?" The answer is clear: the maturity born of sanctification comes only through faith in Christ.

Does this mean that the believer has no personal responsibility to partner with God in this process? Not at all. Scripture is clear about the fact that we each have a part to play in choosing to surrender our will to God on a daily basis. We are told in Galatians 5:16 that we must "walk by the Spirit, and [we] will not carry out the desire of the flesh." We are also told in Romans 12:1–2 that we should partner with God in this process by presenting ourselves to Him as a living sacrifice. Finally, Philippians 2:12–13 offers us the clearest proposition in regard to this partnership:

> So then, my beloved, just as you have always obeyed, not as in my presence only, but now much more in my absence, work out your salvation with fear and trembling; for it is God who is at work in you, both to will and to work for His good pleasure.

We are told to "work out our salvation" not by straining to do more but by humbling ourselves before God and trusting Him to work in us both to will and to act, because God finds great pleasure in this partnership with us.

We are told that God's work in us will have two parts: First, to will. That means that God will work in our desires to persuade us of His good intentions, but we must give Him an invitation to do this work in our will. Second, God will work in us and through us as we surrender to His Spirit's promptings and callings so that we will work, or serve Him, according to His purpose. It is in this fashion and partnership with God that the work of regeneration, or sanctification, takes place in the believer.

14

The Church

The church in the New Testament is that group of people who have given themselves to Christ and joined together collectively to worship and serve Him. They are the outward manifestation of the living Christ, birthed and empowered at Pentecost. The word most often used in the original language of the New Testament to describe the church is the word *ekklésia*.

When introducing his letters, Paul most often chose this word *ekklésia* to define those to whom he was writing. He addressed his letter to the Corinthian believers, "To the church of God which is at Corinth" (1 Cor. 1:2). He did the same when writing to other believers, such as those in the region of Galatia. He wrote in Galatians 1:2, "To the churches of Galatia," and he did this again when he wrote to the believers in Thessalonica. So Paul used this word *ekklésia* to refer to a local group of Christians in fellowship. The church could include large areas such as Galatia or small house churches such as those meeting in the home of Priscilla and Aquila, to whom Paul also addressed a greeting, mentioning those in "the church that is in their house" (Rom. 16:5).

John used the same word *ekklésia* in his letter of Revelation. In chapters 1–3 John addresses himself to seven churches, or *ekklésia*. So we have a broad range of use with this word *ekklésia*, but each time it references a church, because the *ekklésia* is comprised of Christian believers. Each of these groups mentioned in Scripture varied in size, and that was never addressed as an issue, so we might say that a church can be ten, one hundred or ten thousand people. Each church met in different styles and sizes of buildings, which also made no difference, because to the early apostles a church was made up of those who had given themselves over to following the Lord Jesus Christ and Him alone.

One Body United in Christ

That the apostles would address all these groups as the church indicates their perception that the church was universal in nature. The church certainly wasn't seen as an organization but as an active and living organism. This is what Jesus had in mind when He declared, "I will build My church" (Matt. 16:18). This church would consist of one body, us, and one head, Christ, according to Ephesians 5:23: "Christ also is the head of the church, He Himself being the Savior of the body." With Christ as its head, the church becomes the representation of Christ and His work on the earth. The church is universal in nature in that it includes people from every tribe, tongue and nation who desire to enter into Christ's death and saving grace and then live in those realities here on Earth.

This brings us to some of the practical discussions that must take place when defining the church, for the church is not a service club that people can join like the Rotary Club or the Kiwanis Club. These clubs are noble groups that care for others, but the church is far different than a service club. The church is the living representation of Jesus, empowered by His Spirit to do His works, called out of the world and into the body of Christ. Paul wrote as much in 2 Corinthians 6:14–18 when he stated,

> Do not be bound together with unbelievers; for what partnership have righteousness and lawlessness, or what fellowship has light with darkness? Or

> what harmony has Christ with Belial, or what has a believer in common with an unbeliever? Or what agreement has the temple of God with idols? For we are the temple of the living God; just as God said, "I will dwell in them and walk among them; and I will be their God, and they shall be My people. Therefore, come out from their midst and be separate," says the Lord. "And do not touch what is unclean; and I will welcome you. And I will be a father to you, and you shall be sons and daughters to Me," says the Lord Almighty.

This concept of coming out to come in was a radical one in the New Testament. It included not just Jews leaving their Jewish traditions to worship in this new covenant that God had created in Christ, but it included Gentiles leaving their old ways and walking anew as well. The most radical aspect of this proposition was that these Jews and Gentiles were now called to walk together in God's church. In Romans 9:24–26 Paul described this relationship:

> He also called [us], not from among Jews only, but also from among Gentiles. As He says also in Hosea, "I will call those who were not My people, 'My people,' and her who was not beloved, 'beloved.' And it shall be that in the place where it was said to them, 'you are not My people,' there they shall be called sons of the living God."

This new group of believers comprising the church was marked with certain distinctions that much of the church of today has lost. She was, according to Ephesians 5:25–27, to be holy, pure and undefiled:

Christ also loved the church and gave Himself up for her, so that He might sanctify her, having cleansed her by the washing of water with the word, that He might present to Himself the church in all her glory, having no spot or wrinkle or any such thing; but that she would be holy and blameless.

The terms *holy* and *blameless* are not used nearly as often as they should be to describe the church of today. We, the people of God, have in many instances lost the innocence that Christ intends us to live in. The good news remains, however, that He is committed to His work in His bride: "God willed to make known what is the riches of the glory of this mystery among the Gentiles, which is Christ in you, the hope of glory" (Col. 1:27). The hope of the church is not in cleaning herself up but in trusting again that the mystery of Christ in us will be fulfilled unto this hope of glory.

When we talk of the church, we speak of more than one local fellowship. We speak of the interconnectedness of all those who make up the church throughout the earth. This includes the local body of believers, but it is not limited to just this one small group. When any person on Earth surrenders himself or herself to the Lord, that person becomes a part of His church. As Paul says in 1 Corinthians 12:12–13, we are all members of one another:

> For even as the body is one and yet has many members, and all the members of the body, though they are many, are one body, so also is Christ. For by one Spirit we were all baptized into one body, whether Jews or Greeks, whether slaves or free, and we were all made to drink of one Spirit.

We are all gifted by the Holy Spirit for service and ministry, as

Paul goes on to say in verses 14–25 of 1 Corinthians 12. These gifts are diverse and are meant to be used to build up the church. Each member of the church is gifted differently, and no one person has all the gifts of the Spirit. Thus, God has intentionally built into the church interdependence on one another and a natural interconnectedness that is necessary for the church to be healthy. This picture is summed up by Paul:

> Speaking the truth in love, we are to grow up in all aspects into Him who is the head, even Christ, from whom the whole body, being fitted and held together by what every joint supplies, according to the proper working of each individual part, causes the growth of the body for the building up of itself in love. (Eph. 4:15–16)

So we see that the church is to be unified, loving and supportive of one another. This can only happen when the Holy Spirit is at work, breaking down the dividing walls that we erect, such as nationality, race, social status and so on. Paul clarifies this in Colossians 3:11–14:

> There is no distinction between Greek and Jew, circumcised and uncircumcised, barbarian, Scythian, slave and freeman, but Christ is all, and in all. So, as those who have been chosen of God, holy and beloved, put on a heart of compassion, kindness, humility, gentleness and patience; bearing with one another, and forgiving each other, whoever has a complaint against anyone; just as the Lord forgave you, so also should you. Beyond all these things put on love, which is the perfect bond of unity.

This unity led those in the early church to go so far as to disregard their personal property and allow their goods to become common property.

The Church and Israel

The church has at times been caught in theological disputes regarding her proper place in the prophetic material of both the Old and the New Testaments. It is easy, as one reads Old Testament prophecies, to allow Israel to swallow up the church. It is just as easy to allow literal Israel to be swallowed up by many New Testament prophecies. Some of the Old Testament prophetic declarations that were thought to be for Israel were fulfilled in the church. We see this in Romans 9:24–25, which is drawn from Hosea 2:23 and seemed to point to literal Israel until Paul used these words to confirm this prophecy's fulfillment in the church. This also happened with Joel 2:28, which was quoted in Acts 2:17 as pertaining to the church.

This should not cause one to disregard the reality that a literal Israel is also found in the New Testament, as Romans 11:26 declares: "All Israel will be saved." The church is in many ways the new Israel—the book of Romans is clear about that. But at the same time the Scriptures are clear that Israel also has a special place in the future of the body of Christ.

The Called-out Ones

The role of the church is multifaceted. It includes evangelism, which is sharing the heart of God as Acts 1:8 commands; edification, or the building up of believers, which is repeatedly taught throughout the New Testament; fellowship; worship and care for others. Most of these functions can be seen in Acts 2:42, which states that the early church was dynamically engaged in these activities: "They were continually devoting themselves to the apostles' teaching and to fellowship, to the breaking of bread and to prayer."

The church was also marked by a willingness to serve others. This is born out of the heart of Jesus when He declared that He had come to serve and not to be served (see Matt. 20:28). Unfortunately, the church hasn't always been in the business of serving others but has often demanded that others serve her.

This can be reflected in the type of government that is set up in a church. The episcopal form of church rulership (not to be confused with the Episcopal church) lends itself to this problem of asking others to serve the organization rather than leading the church to serve others. It is a top-down hierarchy, which historically has failed to birth servant-hearted Christians. The people are ruled by bishops, cardinals and ultimately, for Catholics, the Pope.

On the other hand, some systems of church government seem far better suited to building servant-hearted believers. The presbyterian system (again, not just the Presbyterian church) places authority in an office but in a far different fashion than the episcopal system does. In a presbyterian system elders rule over the local congregation, which is a biblical practice, and these elders are selected from among the people. Authority rests in the local session, or board, which sends representatives to a general assembly. The local pastor is called by the session and confirmed by the area presbytery, or a group of leaders.

A third form of church government, the congregational system, stresses the role of the individual and doesn't have any form of outside authority. In this system the church is, as it says, run by the congregation. The congregation decides on its pastor as well as on its building and the church's direction. We see this form of government in the book of Acts (6:1–6, 14:21–23, 15:1–31) when the church was selecting deacons and elders and also dealing with important theological issues. This form of government guards against a spirit of lording over others, something Jesus warned us not to do, and it releases the believer to full participation in the ministry. The Scriptures are not directive concerning the type of system that we should use, so it must be remembered that diversity is a blessing and that unity does not equal uniformity in such issues.

In summary, this dynamic and ever-changing gathering or assembly of people to whom God has entrusted His kingdom is His church. Its members are literally the "called ones," or the "called-out ones"—that is what the word *ekklésia* actually means. *Ek* means "out" in Greek, and *kaleó* means "called." So this gathering of God's people that we refer to as the church today is actually the gathering of God's called-out ones—those who have been called "out of darkness into His marvelous light" (1 Pet. 2:9) and empowered by God's Spirit to have fellowship and unity with the Father and with the Father's people.

15

Baptism

Throughout time and history God has given impartations of life to touch His people and, in the case of baptism, to literally immerse them in His blessing. Unfortunately, baptism, like the Lord's Supper, has suffered immensely under the strain of misrepresentation throughout the church's history.

There are several significantly differing views on the rite of baptism revolving around various questions: Is baptism necessary for one's salvation? May a person who is not saved receive salvation by the act of baptism? What is the purpose or meaning of baptism, and what did the early church, Jesus and the apostles intend for it to represent? Who can be baptized? And certainly one of the most controversial issues regarding baptism is the mode in which it is administered.

As has been the case throughout the church's history, Roman Catholic doctrine has managed to make the act of baptism more mystical and effectual than Scripture allows. For the Catholic church the act of baptism is overemphasized and removed from the heart of the gospel. This has led to a tremendous amount of undue tension surrounding baptism, not to mention a very poorly developed and confusing theology that is intended to support their proposition.

An Outward Sign of an Inward Reality

The apostle Paul provided a good foundation for the discussion of baptism in Romans 6:1–4:

> What shall we say then? Are we to continue in sin so that grace may increase? May it never be! How shall we who died to sin still live in it? Or do you not know that all of us who have been baptized into Christ Jesus have been baptized into His death? Therefore we have been buried with Him through baptism into death, so that as Christ was raised from the dead through the glory of the Father, so we too might walk in newness of life.

Believers have all, as Paul declared, "died to sin." This is, in fact, the doctrine of justification. There is, as the author's use of the aorist tense in this phrase suggests, an instant in which one's faith turns into salvation and he is "baptized" into Christ's death and raised anew in newness of life.

The action of water baptism then becomes the outward sign of this inward change to the newness of life. Our old man, our flesh, is symbolically buried during immersion, and the new man is raised from the water just as Christ was raised from the dead. Baptism, then, is much like the Old Testament ritual of circumcision. In and of itself, circumcision did not offer anyone salvation, but it did represent the internal act of a heart that was circumcised unto the Lord. Colossians 2:11–12 offers us a glimpse of this perspective that likens Old Testament circumcision to New Testament baptism:

> In Him you were also circumcised with a circumcision made without hands, in the removal of the body of the flesh by the circumcision of Christ; having been buried with Him in baptism, in which you were also raised up with Him through faith in the working of God, who raised Him from the dead.

So we see that baptism never saved anyone, and it was never intended to. What it does is outwardly express what the Holy Spirit has inwardly accomplished in sealing the believer into the kingdom.

Clearing Up the Questions

Is it then possible to be saved without being baptized? The biblical answer, devoid of human tradition, is most certainly yes. Jesus declared as much to the thief on the cross next to Him when He told him, "Today you shall be with Me in paradise" (Luke 23:43). Any other conjecture does not stand up to biblical scrutiny. Paul weighed in on this proposition when he was asked by the Philippian jailer, "What must I do to be saved?" (Acts 16:30). He did not say, "Believe and be baptized." He stated clearly, "Believe in the Lord Jesus, and you will be saved" (16:31). To insist that baptism must take place in order for one to be saved is a bit like the Judaizers who followed Paul around declaring that circumcision was necessary for salvation. First Peter 3:21 further amplifies the fact that salvation is by faith alone in the resurrection power of Christ: "Corresponding to that, baptism now saves you—not the removal of dirt from the flesh, but an appeal to God for a good conscience—through the resurrection of Jesus Christ." Peter proclaims that salvation comes from a baptism not in water but in the death and resurrection of Christ.

Who then are we to baptize? The Scriptures are clear on this point: only those who have made a decision to follow Christ are to be baptized. Peter declared in Acts 2:38 that it was those who have repented, turned from their former life and come into the arms of Jesus' forgiveness who should be baptized: "Repent, and each of you be baptized in the name of Jesus Christ." Further, if baptism is an outward sign of an inward change, then, according to Romans 8:9, it is only those who have opened by faith to the indwelling power of the Holy Spirit and experienced rebirth in Christ who should be baptized.

Does this include children? Certainly, as long as they properly understand what baptism is about and can give clear testimony to their salvation. Since there are no inherent aspects of salvation built into the action of baptism, it is certainly not wise nor advisable to baptize infants, who can neither give testimony to any activity of salvation nor discern in their will if they even want to participate in a living relationship with Jesus.

If baptism is not crucial for salvation, then why is it a vital part of a Christian's life? Because Jesus sent us into the world to go "and make disciples of all the nations, baptizing them in the name of the Father and the Son and the Holy Spirit, teaching them to observe all that [He] commanded [us]" (Matt. 28:19–20). We are to make disciples, and part of the activity of discipleship building is baptizing new believers and having them declare publicly what they have experienced privately. This is part of teaching disciples to "observe all" that Jesus commanded, including baptism. There is a supernatural component that attends the act of baptism; the thing that God's Spirit has done inwardly is now publicly displayed outwardly. In other words, what God has done in the spiritual realm is now manifest in the natural realm.

When should baptism take place? Often the church has told new believers that before being baptized they need to grow up in Christ and mature to a point at which it is clear that they have been saved. This proposition flies in the face of biblical authority. More than once we read that as soon as people believed, they were baptized. In Acts 2:38, at the time of Pentecost, we see that Peter declared to those to whom he was preaching, "Repent, and each of you be baptized in the name of Jesus Christ for the forgiveness of your sins." There is no mention here of needing to mature or to prove faithfulness before being baptized. Likewise, the Ethiopian eunuch in Acts 8:35–38 was baptized by Phillip immediately following the opening of his heart to Jesus:

Philip opened his mouth, and beginning from this Scripture he preached Jesus to him. As they went along the road they came to some water; and the eunuch said, "Look! Water! What prevents me from being baptized?" And Philip said, "If you believe with all your heart, you may." And he answered and said, "I believe that Jesus Christ is the Son of God." And he ordered the chariot to stop; and they both went down into the water, Philip as well as the eunuch, and he baptized him.

What method of baptism is acceptable? Again, the scriptures that have been reviewed, including the one immediately preceding this paragraph, clearly demonstrate that immersion in the form of dipping or plunging into the water is preferred. Paul's illustration in Romans 6 (being buried with Christ through baptism into death) certainly wouldn't make sense if sprinkling or touching a person's forehead with water was intended. But in declaring that immersion is the preferred biblical method, there is no biblical text that precludes one from sprinkling or from baptizing a believer in some other fashion than immersion. The need for this flexibility often comes into focus for pastors working in a hospital setting, particularly with those patients who are terminally ill and who make a decision to follow Christ. What are we to do if a person desires to be baptized but has no possible means of being immersed, or, as is often the case, could not survive being immersed in water?

Finally, we have the sticky issue of baptizing children. Clearly, infant baptism is not found in the Scriptures, but at what age do we baptize our young people who have made a confession of faith? There are no clear directives in the Bible, so we are left to discern this issue. First and foremost, if a child can and does make a public profession of faith, we would be wise not to underestimate that confession. It is easy for us as adults to downplay a child's response to the Holy Spirit. Yet we are all aware that there is only one Holy Spirit—there is no junior Holy Spirit for kids. When a child opens his or her heart and will to the Father's, he receives the same impartation of God's Spirit that an adult does, and the child's name is written in the Book of Life. So the issue is not one of fullness of forgiveness and salvation but one of timing. How old is old enough? I would venture to say that when a child can clearly articulate what salvation means to him, the time is right for that child to enter into this marvelously supernatural impartation that Jesus instructs all of His children to embrace.

16

The Lord's Supper

It is hard to imagine the night that Jesus first took the bread and the cup and used them to help transform His little band of followers into His bride, the church. Looking back we can see clearly the beauty and magnitude of life that He was ushering His people into. But those who were present on that first communion night had little understanding of the experience they were undergoing, much less what was about to unfold before them in the next three days.

Unfortunately, the Lord's Supper, with all its beauty and possibility for impartation of life, has historically provided fertile ground for a divisive spirit to enter into the church's life. The battles that have been fought over this issue have been well chronicled. They range from the ecclesiastical to the practical.

The Body and Blood: Literal or Symbolic?

There is no doubt that the Catholic church has been guilty of abusing this sacrament. They have embraced a position that inevitably becomes wounding to the body of Christ. Transubstantiation (the belief that the bread and the cup literally become Jesus' body and blood when one receives them in communion) carries with it a great deal of difficult theological baggage. If one is to believe the admonition in Matthew 26:26 that "Take, eat; this is My body" is a literal command, then one must also do so with "Pluck out your eye," as both

Matthew 5:29 and 18:9 declare, or "Cut off your hand," as Jesus commands in Matthew 5:30.

Certainly a literal translation of the command is not what Christ had in mind. If the bread and the wine were literally the actual body and blood of Jesus, the average person or family wanting to participate in communion would find it impossible. This type of teaching ushers in what is known as sacerdotalism—the idea that the priest alone can consecrate the elements—since who would allow laity to handle such a task as distributing the literal body and blood of Christ? This leaves the average believer minimized and held captive to a priest administering communion. This is not found in the Scriptures. In fact, the opposite is found in 1 Peter 2:9–10, where Peter declares of all believers,

> But you are a chosen race, a royal priesthood, a holy nation, a people for God's own possession, so that you may proclaim the excellencies of Him who has called you out of darkness into His marvelous light; for you once were not a people, but now you are the people of God; you had not received mercy, but now you have received mercy.

The communion meal was clearly intended to create unity within the body, not division. Elevating the rite to a supernatural visitation so that it can only be handled by the "elite" of the priesthood certainly is taking a step backward into the Old Testament and not forward into the new covenant that the death and resurrection of Christ initiated. But this elevation of the priesthood is an obvious outcome of the belief that Christ's literal body and blood are present in communion. This exaltation of priests in and of itself violates the priesthood of the believer that Peter speaks of. John, the author of Revelation, highlights this as well: Christ "has made us to be a kingdom, priests to His God and Father" (Rev. 1:6).

Reformers Martin Luther, Ulrich Zwingli and John Calvin have all wrestled with the place that the sacrament of communion holds in the church's life. Do the bread and wine in and of themselves hold the power to heal? If they do not literally become Christ's flesh and blood, do they inherently possess His supernatural presence? The thought that one actually eats and drinks Christ's flesh and blood is absurd. That one enters into deep communion with the Lord of the supper is not. Jesus certainly promised to be present with those who sought after Him. John 14:23 makes this clear: "If anyone loves Me, he will keep My word; and My Father will love him, and We will come to him and make Our abode with him." Partaking of the Lord's Supper is an act of obedience that lends itself to deep communion and relationship between us and God. It is a symbolic act of surrender and hope for the one who enters into it prayerfully.

Examining Ourselves

The apostle Paul addressed the practical aspects of participating in communion in 1 Corinthians 11:23–34. It is here and here alone that the New Testament offers an extensive look at the early church's participation in the Lord's Supper. In order to comprehend the fullness of this text, we must take a moment to examine it closely.

We are often warned prior to participating in the act of communion that we should examine ourselves. This is certainly true, according to verse 28, which declares, "But a man must examine himself, and in so doing he is to eat of the bread and drink of the cup." However, it is crucial that we understand what we are examining ourselves for. Is it to determine whether or not we are worthy to partake of the elements? We are told of our worthiness in Romans 3:10, that there are "none righteous," and in Isaiah 64:6 that all our righteous acts are but "filthy rags" (KJV). So what are we examining ourselves for?

We are told in 1 Corinthians 11:27 not to partake of the elements in an unworthy manner, which immediately lends to us thinking of all we have done wrong that makes us unworthy. Fortunately, this is not what the apostle had in mind. The believers in Corinth, to whom this command was given, were participating in the Lord's Supper in a thoughtless and hurtful manner. Paul asks them in verse 26 to "proclaim the Lord's death until He comes." It is a bit morbid to proclaim death, but we are told Jesus' death means life for us: "It is expedient for you that one man die for the people, and that the whole nation not perish" (John 11:50). So this death is worth celebrating. But how are we to do that? The answer is prayerfully and thoughtfully.

Communion is a time for us to embrace the grace that was offered to its recipients at the cross. It is not, nor was it ever intended to be, a time in which we examine ourselves to see if we are worthy to participate according to our actions or thoughts that have preceded the communion event.

Verse 27, which cautions us to be careful when we eat or drink "in an unworthy manner," is often misunderstood. The King James Version translates *unworthy* as *unworthily*, and this is unfortunate, because it makes the word seem to apply more to the person than to the action being done. The actual word for *unworthily* is *anaxios*. This word is an adverb that describes an action, not an adjective that describes a person. The word *unworthy* actually has to do with the way the Corinthians were being exclusive of the poor during communion, partaking in a gluttonous and drunken manner and dividing the very heart of what Jesus had died to unite. The phrase "unworthy manner" describes this selfish action that had been taking place in the church, regarding which the apostle asks if he should praise the people for their behavior and then soundly declares, "I will not praise you" (11:22).

The admonishment "Let a man examine himself" (11:28, KJV) isn't a call to deep introspection to determine whether or not we are worthy to partake of communion. It is a call to allow the Holy Spirit to search and renew life, to heal and restore. Paul is asking us whether or not our behavior reflects the grace that we embrace. Are we accepting others the way Christ accepts us?

Communion is a time of grace. Grace giving—Christ's life for ours—and grace getting—receiving His love in our time of need.

Partaking in Remembrance of Christ

So the Lord's Supper confers a spiritual benefit upon those who partake of it. In this sense it is certainly sacramental. But as a sacramental part of the church's life, the obvious question arises as to the frequency and the manner with which we ought to participate in it. At Water of Life we typically celebrate communion once a month. We do this regularly on the third Sunday of each month, for no particular reason. We also celebrate communion at many of our special services, such as Christmas Eve services, nights of prayer and worship and Good Friday and Easter services.

Because of our conviction that each member of the body is to be highly involved in the ministry to the church and is to function in the role of minister, we include the church body in the distribution of the elements. This is done by inviting those who would like to serve the body to come forward to the communion tables and to pass out the elements to the congregation. This action allows those in the body to minister directly to one another.

Some are sure to be offended by such a non-liturgical environment, but at the same time many are blessed and afforded the biblical possibility to minister to one another. The Scriptures clearly do not stipulate any special qualifications regarding who should administer the communion elements. In the same sense, we do not feel bound to use unleavened bread and wine, but we choose to use crackers and grape juice.

Due to the sacramental nature of the Lord's Supper, the event is often surrounded by a reflective attitude of worship, which can and certainly does lend itself to the quietness and thoughtfulness due such an event. However, the Scriptures never limit the church to such an atmosphere. Certainly communion is a time to reflect on the death of Christ and on the cost and payment of our sin, but it can and should be celebrated at different times as a praise-filled and joyous event. This allows for the body of Christ to rejoice in the gift of salvation and to offer the praise and thanksgiving our Father is due at such a time. It is, as Jesus said, an experience that brings to remembrance all that He has and is doing for us. Certainly we have short memories, but conversely communion can and should be celebrated at times with a joyful happiness that declares all our gratefulness to God and is free of a somber and inwardly reflective mood.

17

The Sacraments

The sacraments that are typically celebrated by the Protestant Church are based on those ordinances that Jesus declared His disciples should do. The first is the one-time initiatory rite of baptism, and the second is the ongoing and regular remembrance of communion. According to J. I. Packer's *Concise Theology*, "Sacrament is from the Latin word *sacramentum*, meaning a holy rite in general and in particular a soldier's sacred oath of allegiance." Historically, the Protestant church has practiced the two previously mentioned sacraments of baptism and communion. The Roman Catholic church's sacraments, however, have ranged in number from two to seven, depending on the period of church history and on the ecclesiastical authorities to which one spoke. According to *The International Bible Encyclopedia*, the seven sacraments listed by the Roman Catholic church include "Baptism, Confirmation, the Eucharist [communion], Penance, Extreme Unction, Orders, and Matrimony—a suggestion which was supported by certain fanciful analogies designed to show that seven was a sacred number." However, this list was arbitrary and seems to have been established by no certain principles.

The problem of establishing any list of sacraments is the fact that there are no recognized rules, no verses, no biblical teaching defining what passes for a sacrament. The Reformers, unhappy with the seven sacraments listed by the Vatican, chose—again, rather arbitrarily—to distinguish the sacraments they were going to practice by the commands of Jesus that were clearly marked in the Scriptures and had been followed by His disciples. The Reformers believed these commands of Christ to be "the expressions of divine thoughts, the visible symbols of divine acts."

Why Baptism and Communion?

The justification for placing baptism and communion under the banner of sacraments is found in the way these activities are associated in the New Testament. We find them in close proximity to each other in Acts chapter 2: "Those who had received his word were baptized; and that day there were added about three thousand souls. They were continually devoting themselves to the apostles' teaching and to fellowship, to the breaking of bread and to prayer" (2:41–42). Though the activity of baptizing and partaking are found here, they certainly are not declared to be anything other than the two ordinances that Jesus had set forth for His people.

We find nearly the same arrangement in 1 Corinthians 10:1–4, which says,

> I do not want you to be unaware, brethren, that our fathers were all under the cloud and all passed through the sea; and all were baptized into Moses in the cloud and in the sea; and all ate the same spiritual food; and all drank the same spiritual drink, for they were drinking from a spiritual rock which followed them; and the rock was Christ.

Though baptism is mentioned here as is the partaking of spiritual food, again, there is no clear command that defines these two actions as sacraments. So how did the church arrive at this arrangement?

Expositors clearly recognized that the Old Testament set forth two ordinances for the people of God to follow: Passover and circumcision. These two rites of the old covenant were clearly established by the decree of God. They are also found in the New Testament in close proximity to baptism and communion. For example, we see this in Colossians 2:11–12 and in 1 Corinthians 5:7–8:

> In Him you were also circumcised with a circumcision made without hands, in the removal of the body of the flesh by the circumcision of Christ; having been buried with Him in baptism, in which you were also raised up with Him through faith in the working of God, who raised Him from the dead.
>
> Clean out the old leaven so that you may be a new lump, just as you are in fact unleavened. For Christ our Passover also has been sacrificed. Therefore let us celebrate the feast, not with old leaven, nor with the leaven of malice and wickedness, but with the unleavened bread of sincerity and truth.

The obvious arrangement of the Old Testament ordinances near these two New Testament declarations provides a significant argument for the Reformers. Thus we arrive at their decision to attach sacramental significance to only these two of the seven that have been set forth throughout much of the Roman Catholic Church's history.

God's Purpose for the Sacraments

Both the Catholic church and the Reformers agreed that these ordinances are presented as a means of imparting grace to the people of God. Baptism offers forgiveness (see Acts 2:38), cleansing (see Eph. 5:26) and spiritual renewal (see Col. 2:12). The Lord's Supper is a partaking of the grace of God by participating in the body and blood of Christ (see 1 Cor. 10:16). On these points there was little disagreement between the Reformers and the Catholic church. Their differences were minor compared to the discussion regarding the actual significance of practicing these sacraments.

The Catholics continued to hold fast to their doctrine that the sacraments were efficacious. In other words, they believed that participation in the sacraments alone would benefit the partaker, whether or not he was a believer. The outward acts in and of themselves offered saving benefits to those receiving them.

The Reformed position, however, was clear: the outward action did not inherently contain any life-giving power or authority. The power and authority reside in the Holy Spirit, and He alone imparts to the believing one the new life of Christ and the power to live that life. The condition of the participant and his heart's willingness to open up to the grace and hope of Christ determined the possibility to receive from God, not the act of baptism or communion.

For the Roman Catholic, participation in the sacraments by those who are morally prepared equals a step toward salvation—if the sacrament is administered properly by a qualified priest. So Catholics believe that a person who gets baptized by a priest is actually transformed by the baptism itself. This would likewise be true for one receiving the rite of communion. This doctrine of a priest intermediating between God and people is known as sacerdotalism. It takes the sacraments into a mystical and cultish realm, something God never intended. It removes from the laity any chance of administering the rite of baptism or communion.

Certainly nowhere in the New Testament can one find precedent for this practice. But the Catholic church believes that without a priest to administer the sacraments, a worshiper is doomed to a less-than life in God. As a matter of fact, the extreme Catholic view is that unless one participates in these outward rites, he is doomed to a life without salvation.

In conclusion, the two sacraments that can be clearly defended by the Scriptures are those of baptism and the Lord's Supper. Both may and should be part of a believer's life. Yet in and of themselves, they hold no magical transformative possibility. Instead, the life-giving proposition that both of these rites hold are unfolded when the faith of the participant takes hold of the heart of God and opens up to the Lord's imparting power.

18

Eschatology: The Return of Christ

Eschatology has historically indicated a study of last things. These things include two major arenas. First, eschatology has to do with last things pertaining to individuals. These include physical death and the state immediately following it: eternal life and eternal punishment. Second, eschatology is a study of last things as they pertain to the whole of history. These include political circumstances and situations, social events, and the church and her role in these end-time events. They also include those things that the Bible tells us will unfold immediately following the end of this world as we know it: the second coming of Christ, the resurrection of the dead and the final judgment of all humanity.

All these events have been classified into various categories and interpretations that allow for a systematic study of the book of Revelation and end-time events. Each of these categories reflects a differing interpretation of the biblical information and of how this prophetic literature should be interpreted by readers.

There are four primary categories classifying end-time positions. The first is called the futuristic position, which holds that all biblical prophecy describes events that will take place at the end of the age. Second, the preterist view holds that the prophetic events proclaimed in Scripture have already taken place—that they were fulfilled during the time of the writer of each prophecy. The third position, the historical view, falls somewhere between the first two positions and states that Scripture's prophetic events were future at the time of their writing but that they have been taking place throughout history—some have already unfolded, and others are still before us. Finally, the fourth position holds that all the prophetic material found in Scripture is purely symbolic; it represents multiple events and was never meant to represent specific historical events.

Jesus undoubtedly ushered in a new age with His first coming. He repeatedly declared that the kingdom of God had come upon the earth. He stated in Mark 1:15, "The time is fulfilled, and the kingdom of God is at hand; repent and believe in the gospel." This statement was neither symbolic nor futuristic in its representation, though it included the future unfolding of the kingdom. Jesus made this clear by declaring that it was crucial for believers to remain vigilant concerning His second coming: "Be on the alert then, for you do not know the day nor the hour" (Matt. 25:13). He further stated that He would return and that His people should be ready: "You too, be ready; for the Son of Man is coming at an hour that you do not expect" (Luke 12:40).

This is certainly not just a symbolic admonishment but a warning that the prophetic events found in Scripture are in fact real and ready to unfold as the Father wills. With this in mind, the only position that is firmly biblically supported is the historical view, which believes that these events have been unfolding throughout history and that they will continue to unfold until the end of the age. As certain as this position seems to be, it is not without its difficulties, and this helps to remind Christians that end-time events are not, nor should they be, a test of orthodoxy. There are good, thoughtful and solid Bible teachers who hold varying positions, and these differences should never impact our willingness to foster unity in the body.

Jesus' Second Coming and the Rapture

Having established that the prophecies in the Bible should actually be anticipated, in what fashion might they be fulfilled? Multiple scriptures describe the second coming of Christ as a magnificent and glorious event. Jesus Himself proclaimed in Matthew 24:30–31 that He would come with power and glory:

> The sign of the Son of Man will appear in the sky, and then all the tribes of the earth will mourn, and they will see the Son of Man coming on the clouds of the sky with power and great glory. And He will send forth His angels with a great trumpet and they will gather together His elect from the four winds, from one end of the sky to the other.

Each of the four Gospels carry similar accounts of the second coming of Christ, as does the book of Acts, in which angelic hosts declare, "Men of Galilee, why do you stand looking into the sky? This Jesus, who has been taken up from you into heaven, will come in just the same way as you have watched Him go into heaven" (1:11). The epistles of Paul further expand on the reality of a second coming, particularly 1 Thessalonians 4:15–17, which specifies that Jesus will gather His people unto Himself when He returns:

> For this we say to you by the word of the Lord, that we who are alive and remain until the coming of the Lord, will not precede those who have fallen asleep. For the Lord Himself will descend from heaven with a shout, with the voice of the archangel and with the trumpet of God, and the dead in Christ will rise first. Then we who are alive and remain will be caught up together with them in the clouds to meet

the Lord in the air, and so we shall always be with the Lord.

The fact of a literal, physical second coming of Jesus is biblically undeniable. What remains in question is the timing of such an event. Again, Jesus repeatedly asserted that this was not information that He would or could divulge to His disciples. He stated as much in Mark 13:32–33, following an extended discourse on the end times: "But of that day or hour no one knows, not even the angels in heaven, nor the Son, but the Father alone. Take heed, keep on the alert; for you do not know when the appointed time will come." What Jesus did tell us is that we are to be ready for His return and for the fulfillment of the end of the age. We are told to be watchful, aware of the events that are unfolding around us, and that we are not to be lulled to sleep by the things of this world.

Throughout church history it has been asserted by some that Jesus' second coming took place at Pentecost. Adherents of this belief say that the Scriptures describing Him as being always present, such as Matthew 28:20, "Lo, I am with you always, even to the end of the age," actually indicate that it was Jesus, not the Holy Spirit, who fell on the early disciples. The problem with such a position is simple: far too many of the statements concerning Jesus' second coming were written in the epistles after the Pentecost event.

What will Jesus' second coming look like? Could we miss it, as those who assert that it took place at Pentecost suggest that we have? According to Jesus' statement in Matthew 24:30, this would be impossible. He said, "Then the sign of the Son of Man will appear in the sky, and then all the tribes of the earth will mourn, and they will see the Son of Man coming on the clouds of the sky with power and great glory." The statement "they will see" makes it very clear that Jesus' coming will not be a hidden event but one that the whole of the world will watch.

Though it will be seen worldwide, it will be seen primarily by people who are in great shock and totally surprised. Jesus said that it will be like the days of Noah (see Matt. 24:37) and that people will be caught unaware, as they were in Noah's day:

> They were eating, they were drinking, they were marrying, they were being given in marriage, until the day that Noah entered the ark, and the flood came and destroyed them all. . . . It will be just the same on the day that the Son of Man is revealed. (Luke 17:27, 30)

One of the controversies that continues to surround this end-time event is the question of whether Jesus' return will actually be two events or one. Is the rapture (the removal of all believers from the earth) a separate event from the actual return of Jesus, as many pretribulationists believe it will be, or will Jesus' return and the rapture be one event? In order to sustain the dual-event scenario, the words that are used in the original language describing Christ's return must reflect this fact, and they do not.

There are several terms we find in the Scriptures that describe the second coming. They include *parousia*, *apokalupsis* and *epiphaneia*. An intricate case is made by some that each is used in particular situations to indicate that the rapture and the return of Christ are separate events, but upon close study it appears to be a forced issue. These terms are used interchangeably by Paul in his writings in Titus, 1 Corinthians and 1 Thessalonians as well as in both 1 and 2 Timothy. So to prove a case for two separate events is difficult, and it is biblically easier to see Christ's return and the rapture as one event. But it is important to say that this is far from an open-and-closed case. As stated previously, there are many wise and well-studied biblical teachers who hold to separate events.

The Judgment

Upon Jesus' return what will take place? The bodily resurrection of the dead will occur, both the righteous and the unrighteous, which will be followed by the Day of Judgment. Both the Old and the New Testaments support this position. Daniel 12:2 states, "Many of those who sleep in the dust of the ground will awake, these to everlasting life, but the others to disgrace and everlasting contempt." Matthew 25:31–33 describes Jesus sitting on the throne of judgment at this time:

> When the Son of Man comes in His glory, and all the angels with Him, then He will sit on His glorious throne. All the nations will be gathered before Him; and He will separate them from one another, as the shepherd separates the sheep from the goats; and He will put the sheep on His right, and the goats on the left.

Each of those at the judgment seat will be judged according to his or her life on Earth: "Do not marvel at this; for an hour is coming, in which all who are in the tombs will hear His voice, and will come forth; those who did the good deeds to a resurrection of life, those who committed the evil deeds to a resurrection of judgment" (John 5:28–29). These good deeds do not in and of themselves merit believers a ticket to salvation; they are those things that are set before us after we have been saved by grace, according to Ephesians 2:8–10:

> For by grace you have been saved through faith; and that not of yourselves, it is the gift of God; not as a result of works, so that no one may boast. For we are His workmanship, created in Christ Jesus for good works, which God prepared beforehand so that we would walk in them.

Thus, the judgment will usher in the new age of eternal life and blessing, fulfilling God's eternal desire that His people will be in His presence forever and restoring all that was stolen and lost at the Fall. God's people will worship God before His throne so that they might be His people and He might be their God.

19

Revelation

The doctrine of revelation is born out of the reality that God is infinite and man is not. Therefore, if man is to know God, it must be because God reveals Himself to man. This revelation takes place in multiple and numerous ways, but there are two primary classifications of revelation: general and specific.

General revelation is God communicating to all mankind in all places and at all times, most commonly in the things we see around us in the world. God's special revelation is much more particular and specific. Special revelation is God revealing Himself to individual people through specific communication—powerful deeds in people's lives, God's voice speaking into our lives and, most obviously, through God's living Word.

General Revelation

General revelation has been traditionally considered to come to mankind through three different means: nature, history and the makeup of human beings.

Nature has held people in awe throughout history. The impact on a person of a glimpse of the Grand Canyon or some other natural spectacle can be deep and life impacting. It can and often does make it difficult for a person to deny that there is a creator.

Psalm 19:1–2 declares, "The heavens are telling of the glory of

God; and their expanse is declaring the work of His hands. Day to day pours forth speech, and night to night reveals knowledge." Paul, in Romans 1:19–20, offers a similar look at how general revelation impacts mankind:

> That which is known about God is evident within them; for God made it evident to them. For since the creation of the world His invisible attributes, His eternal power and divine nature, have been clearly seen, being understood through what has been made, so that they are without excuse.

This is certainly the most direct and pointed text in the New Testament concerning the impact of nature and its revelation of God. There are many psalms that are considered nature psalms, but none is as direct in its estimation of nature's impacting presence on mankind as are these verses in Romans.

A second means by which God reveals Himself generally is through history. If God is actually in control of all creation, one ought to be able to see His hand orchestrating events as He works to accomplish certain goals throughout history. This can be seen when one studies the history of Israel.

The third and final type of general revelation is the existence of man himself. As with a wonderfully made watch, it is difficult to believe that man is an accident of nature. The fullness of God's revelation in man is seen in the complex makeup of man's consciousness and in his ability to make moral judgments. It is these two aspects of humankind that set man apart from the rest of creation and reveal to us that man is in indeed made in the image of God. Man's hunger to worship and to believe in the existence of a higher being in and of itself is a picture of general revelation. While this worship is often twisted or broken, it nevertheless reveals the inherent need of man to seek for something higher than what he sees in creation.

Can General Revelation Bring People to Salvation?

There are several assumptions that must be dealt with in the arena of general revelation. In this type of revelation, it is assumed that God has given a glimpse of Himself in all He has created. His ability to create in such varied and intricate detail reveals His love of color and of the beauty He put in life. A second assumption inherent is that man can perceive from this beauty that there is a God. He can read the writing on the wall, as it were, and recognize its author.

The core idea in general revelation is that it is possible for a person to come to a general knowledge of God without ever having been told about Him by another person, without ever having read the Scriptures or without ever having been taught of God by any institution such as the church.

Thomas Aquinas developed this perspective that we know as natural theology as much as anyone. He believed that there were two realms of truth: higher and lower. Higher truth was the realm of grace and thus supernaturally discerned, and lower truth was discovered in the realm of nature. Aquinas believed that everything in the natural realm had a cause—that nothing happened on its own. If things were to move, they must have a cause. Aquinas called this cause that moved all things the Unmoved Mover, or the Necessary Being—whom we know as God. Aquinas also believed in a teleological argument, which focused on the orderliness in the universe. He concluded that the order around us could not possibly be an accident.

Ultimately, these views were arranged into two major categories, or arguments for the existence of God, that developed around nature and history. They became known as the anthropological and the ontological arguments. The anthropological argument deals with man, particularly in the area of morality and ethics. If being good isn't always rewarded in this life—and it is not—then why not be selfish all the time? The answer is that we have an inborn sense that we will one day face judgment and God face to face. This sense of God and of His justice within us, so the argument says, had to have its origin in God. The ontological argument is an argument that takes place within oneself. This argument says that we do not have to go outside or see anything in nature at all—God is simply so great that He is the most conceivable of all beings, and therefore He must exist.

There are several problems with natural theology. First, if God is seen in nature, what are we to think of Him when we see natural disasters that kill hundreds of people? Earthquakes, floods, lightning and such that are often referred to as "acts of God" make this argument less than desirable for many. Then we can find that history hasn't been so kind either. How can one see God in Nazi Germany, in which many evangelical Germans supported Hitler? This was the cause for Karl Barth's strong position that without special revelation—God speaking directly and personally to individuals—it is impossible for a person to know God. Yet Paul declared in Romans 1:18–32 that it was possible and that man would be held accountable because he does have knowledge of God.

Not to be lost in this argument regarding general revelation is the reality that sin and its ability to mar the hearts and minds of men can make them fail to see the revelation of God in His creation. Romans 1:21 alludes to this blindness: "For even though they knew God, they did not honor Him as God or give thanks, but they became futile in their speculations, and their foolish heart was darkened." This text leads one to question how effective general revelation is on a life that is broken and dark.

General revelation, it must be stated, does not bring people to salvation. We never find an argument for such a belief in the Scriptures. What we do see is the reality that those who throw themselves on the mercy of God are in a much better place than those who do not. This is clearly pictured throughout the Old Testament, and Paul seems to assert as much in Acts:

> For while I was passing through and examining the objects of your worship, I also found an altar with this inscription, "TO AN UNKNOWN GOD." Therefore what you worship in ignorance, this I proclaim to you. The God who made the world and all things in it, since He is Lord of heaven and earth, does not dwell in temples made with hands. (17:23–24)

Paul seemed to indicate that what these people worshiped in ignorance could be defined in the person of Christ. This type of salvation, if it is to be called that—in which one worships God without knowing who He is—is what we see throughout the Old Testament. A person's salvation, both before and after Jesus lived on Earth, is based only on what Christ did on the cross, even when the person is not conscious of that work.

At a minimum it can be stated that general revelation is the starting point for many people to come to know God. But without special revelation, mankind is left to grope through much of the darkness that sin has left in this world.

Special Revelation

Special revelation is the means by which God manifests Himself to particular people at specific times and places. Special revelation became necessary once sin entered this world, for without it mankind's eyes are dimmed by sin and unable to see the fullness of God. General revelation is inferior to special revelation in its ability to reveal both the fullness of God and the salvation of God. But special revelation does build upon general revelation and often uses it as a starting point to help man begin an intimate relationship with God.

Special revelation is personal and therefore deals with the person of God. This is why God told Moses His name when Moses asked:

"I AM WHO I AM" (Exod. 3:14). It is also why Scripture is not vague but specific. The Bible is not a book of general thoughts but of specific insights into the heart and person of God.

This kind of revelation is seen throughout the ages in the mighty deeds of God in individual lives. The Bible speaks of these deeds over and over, because they reveal God to us. Whether it is the parting of the Red Sea or Jesus raising Lazarus from the dead, events such as these show us a personal God.

Much is made throughout Scripture of God's divine speech, as well, for it too holds the key to who God is. The Bible often says, "The word of the Lord came to me, saying . . ." because it is in His spoken word that God allows us to know Him. His voice may be audible, or it may be inaudible, a silent inward knowing that allows one to come into personal contact with God. But whether audible or inaudible, God reveals Himself to us through His voice in a very specific way. Jesus made this point in John 10:27–28 when He stated, "My sheep hear My voice, and I know them, and they follow Me; and I give eternal life to them, and they will never perish; and no one will snatch them out of My hand."

Finally, we have the special revelation of God in His written Word and in the incarnation of His Son. It is here that we come into the most intimate and personal relationship with God through His living Word, His Son Jesus Christ. We read and we know, through the power of the Holy Spirit firsthand, the intimate touch of God. It is in His Word that God reveals Himself to mankind with a sure sense that His revelation to us is and always has been about patching the rupture that sin caused between God and man. It is about relationship with a loving God who has often and repeatedly revealed Himself through many different modes and means as the one creator and Redeemer of the world.

20

Providence

The doctrine of providence defines the continuing work of God in His creation. This takes place in several forms and shapes, including God's dealings with our daily lives, His dealings with nature and His overarching dealings with all creation.

Providence is typically thought to have two roles in creation. First, the ongoing preservation of creation—the sustaining and undergirding work that God does to maintain creation. The second is God's direct hand in shaping the events of history. This action fulfills the course of history as God desires it to be fulfilled, so it is called God's government, or His governing work.

God's Ongoing Preservation of Creation

The first aspect of providence, that of preservation, or the maintaining role of God in His creation, takes on several different aspects. Nehemiah 9:6 states,

> You alone are the LORD. You have made the heavens, the heaven of heavens with all their host, the earth and all that is on it, the seas and all that is in them. You give life to all of them and the heavenly host bows down before You.

Paul also describes God's governing hand in Colossians 1:17: "He is before all things, and in Him all things hold together," and Hebrews says that Jesus upholds "the universe by the power of his word." Thus, it is obvious that deists, who hold that God set the world in motion and then let it unfold as it would, are at odds with the biblical picture of God playing an active role in His creation.

Throughout the Old Testament we see God's hand as active in the affairs of Israel and the people of God therein. From Joseph, who served Pharaoh in Egypt in order to provide food for the people of God, to Daniel, who was thrown into the lions' den, to Moses, who was put afloat in the river to circumvent Pharaoh's decree to kill all the newborn boys, we see God's sovereign hand at work.

Jesus spoke at length about God's work of preservation:

> For this reason I say to you, do not be worried about your life, as to what you will eat or what you will drink; nor for your body, as to what you will put on. Is not life more than food, and the body more than clothing? Look at the birds of the air, that they do not sow, nor reap nor gather into barns, and yet your heavenly Father feeds them. Are you not worth much more than they? And who of you by being worried can add a single hour to his life? And why are you worried about clothing? Observe how the lilies of the field grow; they do not toil nor do they spin, yet I say to you that not even Solomon in all his glory clothed himself like one of these. But if God so clothes the grass of the field, which is alive today and tomorrow is thrown into the furnace, will He not much more clothe you? You of little faith! (Matt. 6:25–30)

This text makes it clear that God is not a distant and removed ruler, as the deists would declare. Not only does He have His hand in men's lives and daily affairs, but He is intimately acquainted with all our needs and desires. Nor is there any doubt that the Bible teaches that without God's sustaining hand, creation has no ability to continue to exist. In this passage Jesus speaks first to the crucial issues of life, food, clothing and housing. Then He enlarges our perspective by stating that if God cares so for the rest of His creation, how or why would He not care for those made in His image?

This intimacy that God has toward His creation is at the heart of His desire to have relationship with people. In John 10:27–29 Jesus describes the sovereign care of the Father for those who would seek Him:

> My sheep hear My voice, and I know them, and they follow Me; and I give eternal life to them, and they will never perish; and no one will snatch them out of My hand. My Father, who has given them to Me, is greater than all; and no one is able to snatch them out of the Father's hand.

Here the overarching protection of God for those He calls His own comes into view. But it is crucial to state that this in no way precludes those whom God loves from suffering and struggling while on Earth, as the Scripture clearly teaches. Both Jesus and Peter treat this issue in depth. Jesus spoke to it in Matthew 24:15–31, where He said,

> Pray that your flight will not be in the winter, or on a Sabbath. For then there will be a great tribulation, such as has not occurred since the beginning of the world until now, nor ever will. Unless those days had been cut short, no life would have been saved; but for the sake of the elect those days will be cut short. (24:20–22)

Likewise, 1 Peter 1:6 says, "In this you greatly rejoice, even though now for a little while, if necessary, you have been distressed by various trials." It is clear that as much as God is at work among us, He will not always, or even often, save us from struggles and trials.

Why is God's preservation important to our daily lives? Because it offers us hope in the midst of struggles and peace in the middle of trials. If we know that God is intimately acquainted with all our ways and actively at work in our midst, then we have a confidence that no matter what we come up against, God will be there. The psalmist understood this well:

> I will say to the LORD, "My refuge and my fortress, my God, in whom I trust!" For it is He who delivers you from the snare of the trapper and from the deadly pestilence. He will cover you with His pinions, and under His wings you may seek refuge; His faithfulness is a shield and bulwark. You will not be afraid of the terror by night, or of the arrow that flies by day; of the pestilence that stalks in darkness, or of the destruction that lays waste at noon. (Ps. 91:2–6)

The kind of confidence that is exuded in this passage can only come from an eternal perspective that believes that God is an active agent in the affairs of mankind. He is a God whom we can trust to cover us from threat. He is a refuge for us from the struggles we face and a protector of those who seek His face.

God's Governing Hand in History

The other critical aspect of God's providence is the governing activity He holds. This governing has to do with the unfolding of His plans in creation. This means that God functions with all of history and mankind in mind, and He steers events to an ultimate goal that He has in mind. God's governing activity covers a myriad of areas, including nature, animal life and nations. Scripture is clear that God not only created nature but that He still rules over it today. We see this in the Old Testament:

> I know that the LORD is great and that our Lord is above all gods. Whatever the LORD pleases, He does, in heaven and in earth, in the seas and in all deeps. He causes the vapors to ascend from the ends of the earth; who makes lightnings for the rain, who brings forth the wind from His treasuries. (Ps. 135:5–7)

We see God's providence over nature in action in the New Testament through the life of Jesus. In Luke 8:23–24 we read,

> As they were sailing along He fell asleep; and a fierce gale of wind descended on the lake, and they began to be swamped and to be in danger. They came to Jesus and woke Him up, saying, "Master, Master, we are perishing!" And He got up and rebuked the wind and the surging waves, and they stopped, and it became calm.

Certainly this kind of miraculous intervention in the affairs of men startles those who experience it. Luke 8:25 records the disciples' response to Jesus' miraculous providential ability:

> He said to them, "Where is your faith?" They were fearful and amazed, saying to one another, "Who then is this, that He commands even the winds and the water, and they obey Him?"

Matthew 5:45 enlarges upon Jesus' governing power, declaring that God's providence covers both those who love Him and those who don't, "for He causes His sun to rise on the evil and the good, and sends rain on the righteous and the unrighteous." In many cases this includes those who are estranged from God, including the nations of the world. In this we see another facet of God's government: His interaction with the rulers and powers of this world. Daniel 2:21 says, "It is He who changes the times and the epochs; He removes kings and establishes kings."

If God is so caring and protecting, how are we to perceive those things that appear to be accidents? Proverbs 16:33 declares that there is no such thing as an accident for those who seek after God: "The lot is cast into the lap, but its every decision is from the LORD." Paul, in Romans 8:28, confidently states, "We know that God causes all things to work together for good to those who love God, to those who are called according to His purpose."

The question could certainly be posed that if God is in control and overseeing His creation, then isn't He responsible for sin in the world and all its results? The Bible's answer is that God is never the cause of sin: "Let no one say when he is tempted, 'I am being tempted by God'; for God cannot be tempted by evil, and He Himself does not tempt anyone" (James 1:13). But if sin isn't caused by God, how does God relate to sin in His creation?

First, there are times when He prevents sin. Such was the case when He gave Abimelech a dream so that he wouldn't take Sarah as his wife (see Gen. 20:3). Second, there are times when God doesn't stop sin, even though He hates it. This would be the case with divorce. Jesus said in Matthew 19:8 that God allowed Moses to permit divorce because of the "hardness of heart" in the people. Third, God sometimes uses sin to accomplish His purposes. This is what happened to Joseph (see Gen. 45). What was meant for evil was turned to good, as it was at the cross. Finally, God can and does at times limit sin. This was the case with Job when God limited Satan's work in his life by setting a boundary, declaring to the devil, "He is in your power, only spare his life" (Job 2:6).

In all of God's providence, nothing impacts His will as do the prayers of His people. We are told in James 5:16, "The prayer of a righteous man is powerful and effective" (NIV). Scripture is clear that God is willing to partner with mankind in His governing if people will come to Him in prayer. It was Jesus who taught His disciples to pray for their daily bread and for their release and deliverance from the evil one; and it was Jesus who taught that we should ask and keep asking, knock and keep knocking, believing that we will receive if we are persistent in prayer (see Luke 11:8–10).

God's providence is sure and good. He is willing to partner with mankind and to use us to fulfill His destiny. What higher call could we want?

21

Scripture

The written Word of God is more than a book on life—it is the book of life. Steering and directing those who would seek its wisdom and counsel, the Bible is our road map to destiny. The Scriptures have been supernaturally influenced, or inspired, by the Spirit of God to inspire, impart and renew life in us. They contain the written revelation of the living Word. The Bible was written by men who were moved by the hand of God, inspired to record the Word of God for all time. If revelation is the unveiling of the truth of God, then inspiration is the preserving of that revelation.

Inspiration is a theology that gives us the assurance that when the message of special revelation was received from God and passed on in the form of Scripture, it was passed on as the truth God intended it to be. But the topic of inspiration seems to be very subjective. How can we know that the written word was actually the Word of the Lord? Why can't someone continue to add to the Bible today?

The Inspired Word of God

With regard to whether or not the Bible is the inspired Word of God, the best place to start is with the claims it makes about itself. Second Peter 1:20–21 offers this defense of the Old Testament prophetic writings:

> But know this first of all, that no prophecy of Scripture is a matter of one's own interpretation, for no prophecy was ever made by an act of human will, but men moved by the Holy Spirit spoke from God.

On the surface it may seem to be circular reasoning to state that a book defends itself, but the truth is that Peter, one of the earliest church fathers, believed that the Old Testament spoke the Word of God through "men moved by the Holy Spirit."

The apostle Paul offered a similar defense of the Scriptures in 2 Timothy 3:16–17: "All Scripture is inspired by God and profitable for teaching, for reproof, for correction, for training in righteousness; so that the man of God may be adequate, equipped for every good work."

It may be one thing for Peter and Paul to make such declarations, but there are several instances of these same men employing Old Testament texts, the very Scripture they were defending, in their own preaching. For example, in Acts 1:16 we see that Peter said to a large crowd, "Brethren, the Scripture had to be fulfilled, which the Holy Spirit foretold by the mouth of David concerning Judas, who became a guide to those who arrested Jesus." He then quoted from Psalms 69:25 and 109:8 as the fulfillment of Judas' fate. How could Peter do such a thing if he did not believe that the Old Testament was the inspired Word of God?

Jesus Himself often quoted from the Old Testament during His ministry. He began His public ministry with a reading from the scroll of Isaiah:

> "The Spirit of the Lord is upon Me, because He anointed Me to preach the gospel to the poor. He has sent Me to proclaim release to the captives, and recovery of sight to the blind, to set free those who are oppressed, to proclaim the favorable year of the

Lord." And He closed the book, gave it back to the attendant and sat down; and the eyes of all in the synagogue were fixed on Him. And He began to say to them, "Today this Scripture has been fulfilled in your hearing." (Luke 4:18–21)

After reading the prophecy of Isaiah, Jesus then validated its inspiration by stating that it had in fact been realized in that meeting. This was only one of several instances in which Jesus used the Old Testament Scriptures. Another instance was during His forty days of fasting and prayer, when He was tempted by Satan. Jesus' response as a defense to Satan and his temptations was to repeatedly offer an Old Testament text. It is important to note as well that in the many times when Jesus rebuked or corrected the religious leaders of His time about wrong teaching and wrong interpretation of these same Old Testament texts, He never corrected their view that these texts were the inspired revelation of God.

What Is Inspiration?

Yet even with all this information available, biblical inspiration has undergone repeated attacks by both believers and non-believers. Questions pertaining to inspiration often question the Scripture's uniformity, its accuracy, the instrument or person involved in the writing of it and the writer's relationship to the inspiration. This last question is particularly interesting, as it deals with the question of how the human writer fits into the scheme of the Holy Spirit anointing a man for the purpose of inspiration. Was the author chosen because he was a prophet or an apostle or held some other office? If the person held an office, then one could reason that anything he wrote would be inspired, could he not? Or is it possible that the inspiration was only applicable to the Scripture that he was writing?

Several theories speak to these questions. For starters, there are the intuition illumination theories. Was the author under intuition in writing the Scriptures, or was he under illumination? If intuition, then human agency and natural gifting were responsible for the result; if illumination, then the Holy Spirit heightened the writer's normal powers.

The verbal theory contends that the influence of the Holy Spirit extends all the way to the selection of each word that is written, and the dictation theory, as its name suggests, asserts that inspiration is in reality dictation from God—in other words, the Holy Spirit told the author exactly what to write, word for word, and left no room for the author's personality or influence.

The truth lies somewhere between these differing propositions. We know that dictation did in fact occur at different points and times in the development of Scripture. Several of the Old Testament's prophetic authors take no issue with the fact that God spoke, or revealed, and they simply wrote down what He told them. John describes such a scenario in the book of Revelation (see Rev. 1:10–11). We also know, however, that there were times when the authors' armor came off, so to speak, and their humanity is revealed in the Scriptures. We see this when Paul rebuked Peter for his treatment of Gentiles (see Gal. 2:11–21), so there is no doubt that Peter, one of the authors and writers of Scripture, was in reality fallible at times.

Jesus seemed to indicate that inspiration extended to every word of Scripture but that it also flowed through the instrumentation of the author and his unique personality. Jesus' comments about marriage illuminate this idea for us:

> Have you not read that He who created them from the beginning made them male and female, and said, "For this reason a man shall leave his father and mother and be joined to his wife, and the two shall become one flesh"? So they are no longer two, but one flesh. What therefore God has joined together, let no man separate. (Matt. 19:4–6)

Jesus attributes this quotation from Genesis 2:24 to God, yet in the original it is not attributed to God. This leaves us to assume that Jesus believed that God had spoken this statement word for word to the author and inspired him to write it. We can conclude that the writers of Scripture were directly inspired by God to write the precise words He wanted written at the exact point He wanted them written. Some of the words were dictated and others verbally inspired through the instrumentation of the individual author, which is why Luke's style was different than, say, Paul's.

The Inerrancy of the Scriptures

Does the fact that God used men in writing the Scriptures allow for the Bible to be considered inerrant, and if so, how does that work?

Inerrancy goes a step further than inspiration by stating not just that Scripture comes from God but that Scripture is entirely truthful. For some that means that the Bible is an accurate scientific tool, for others it is a history book. Still others believe that it is truthful but that it was never meant to be a historical document or a scientific book—it was meant to convey a spiritual message first and foremost. And others hold that inerrancy consists of the fact that the Bible simply accomplishes its purpose.

The bottom line here is simple. Is the Bible believable? What is one to do with some of the obvious issues of discrepancy? All four of the Gospels contain differing verbiage when describing the inscription that hung over Jesus' cross. And what do we make of the differing dates and numbers that don't match up in Scripture? Inerrancy declares that in spite of these seeming mistakes, the Bible correctly interprets the information in a way that the culture at the time of its writing would have found to be truthful and accurate in view of the affairs that the Scriptures dealt with.

The Bible relates many stories and situations that although true are not literally concise. But this certainly does not make such accounts untrue. Far from it. All that the Bible purports to do is to report things accurately. The Bible's assertions are fully true when taken in their context and judged in accordance with the purpose for which they were written. That is why Numbers 25:9 can report that 24,000 died by the plague and Paul can write in 1 Corinthians 10:8 that 23,000 died. Both are approximations, and for the purpose for which they were shared, they are accurate and should be regarded as true.

We do the same in our culture. When asked what we paid for our home, we answer $250,000, and yet precisely we paid $248,558. Such an answer would never bring accusations of lying. The number stated is sufficient for the context of buying homes. However, if the IRS asked the price of our home and we gave an approximate answer, it would then be a lie.

What does all this mean? The principle of inerrancy believes that in relating truth in the Scriptures, all the specifics that need to be recorded will be included and that whatever statements the Bible makes are fully truthful when correctly interpreted in the context in which they were written and for the purpose they were meant to convey.

Ultimately, this means that the Bible carries the same authority and significance as a direct word from God to us. The Bible is God's message, and it should command the same attention as if God were here and speaking directly to us. According to Jesus, the Holy Spirit promises to bring supernatural comprehension and insight to those who ask Him to teach them the heart and Word of God:

> The Helper, the Holy Spirit, whom the Father will send in My name, He will teach you all things, and bring to your remembrance all that I said to you. (John 14:26)

It is vital for us to remember, when all is said and done, that the Holy Spirit, not man, is the author of the Bible. The Holy Spirit will never violate the Word that He has written, so when we read the Scriptures, we can move into God's presence with confidence and trust God's Spirit to speak to us personally, and we can then confirm and clarify God's voice within us in His written Word. When we do this, we find a treasure of life, healing, renewal and redeeming power in God's Word.

Part 2
Position Papers

The Ministry and Gifts of the Holy Spirit

One of the greatest blessings the Bible offers a believer is the promise of the Father. This promise is referred to initially in Luke 24:49 and again in Acts 1:4, 2:33 and 2:38, in Galatians 3:14 and in Ephesians 1:13. These verses create an excitement and an anticipation of possibility and life fulfilled for all those who are counted as New Testament believers. Much of the book of Acts as well as many of the Epistles center around the work and ministry of the Holy Spirit.

Yet the work of the Holy Spirit is likely the most misunderstood ministry in the entire Bible. The Holy Spirit's work is often abused or misused, creating a fear that keeps many who are hungry for a deeper and more meaningful walk with God at a distance. Much of the church has assigned the work of the Holy Spirit to certain denominations or groups of believers, a decision that insulates them from the challenge of working through all that it takes to have a Spirit-filled walk with Jesus.

There is no question that the work of the Spirit can be difficult to understand. His activity is often clouded in mystery. Yet there are many practical examples in the Bible of the Spirit working in the day-to-day affairs of believers, bringing life and passion as well as balance and integrity to ministry. The truth is, much of the work of the Spirit isn't nearly as mystical as many Christians would like people to believe, though it is all certainly supernatural. The great Bible scholar R. A. Torrey once said,

> The secret of effectual living is knowing the power of the Spirit through the Word. The secret of effec-

tual service is using the Word in the power of the Spirit. There are some who seek to magnify the Spirit, but neglect the Word. This will not do at all. Fanaticism, baseless enthusiasm, and wildfire are the result. Others seek to magnify the Word, but largely ignore the Spirit. Neither will this do. It leads to dead orthodoxy, truth without life and power. The true course is to recognize the instrumental power of the Word through which the Holy Spirit works, and the living, personal power of the Holy Spirit who acts through the Word.

Clarifying the Ministry of the Holy Spirit

Christians often hunger for a deeper and more meaningful relationship with the Father, one that is full of His interaction with them. This is the work of the Spirit, the work that 1 Corinthians 12, 13 and 14 speak of—a releasing of charismata or spiritual gifts to empower believers into God's presence. Unfortunately, we have all witnessed or heard about the misuse and abuse of these gifts, which causes many to fear the Spirit's ministry. It is important to say at the outset of this discussion that people, including many Christians, tend to abuse whatever it is that God gives to bless us. We have often abused the life-giving grace of the cross, taking advantage of the death and resurrection of Christ. Fortunately, God doesn't withdraw grace due to humans abusing it. In like manner, when we abuse the gifts and ministry of the Holy Spirit, we are taught in the Word to correct our behavior, not to do away with the Spirit's ministry.

The Baptism of the Holy Spirit

The book of Romans makes it clear that all believers receive the Holy Spirit at their rebirth:

However, you are not in the flesh but in the Spirit,
if indeed the Spirit of God dwells in you. But if
anyone does not have the Spirit of Christ, he does
not belong to Him. (Rom. 8:9)

The book of Acts teaches that after that initial sealing of the Spirit, there is still a deeper work of the Spirit to be done in every believer's life. Many call that work the baptism of the Holy Spirit. The Scriptures refer to this work as the "filling," "renewing," "refreshing" and "baptizing" of the Holy Spirit. What is abundantly clear is the ongoing need of all Christians to be impacted by the Holy Sprit—to be touched, filled, baptized and renewed experientially by the Holy Spirit as the disciples were on the day of Pentecost:

And when the day of Pentecost had come, they
were all together in one place. And suddenly there
came from heaven a noise like a violent, rushing
wind, and it filled the whole house where they were
sitting. And there appeared to them tongues as of
fire distributing themselves, and they rested on each
one of them. And they were filled with the Holy
Spirit and began to speak with other tongues, as the
Spirit was giving them utterance. (Acts 2:1–4)

But you will receive power when the Holy Spirit has
come upon you; and you shall be My witnesses both
in Jerusalem, and in all Judea and Samaria, and even
to the remotest part of the earth. (Acts 1:8)

The Purpose and Power of God's Spirit

At Water of Life, we do not believe that there are two tiers of believers in Christianity: those who are baptized in the Holy Spirit and those who are not. When we create this distinction as a marker of spiritual maturity, we do a fundamental disservice to all involved. Rather, we believe that the baptism of the Holy Spirit is given to all believers primarily to empower them to do ministry.

The book of Acts makes this very clear. The disciples were told to remain in the Upper Room in prayer until the Father visited them with power from on high. This power was never meant to be exercised in a way that brought some into deeper relationship with the Father while holding others out. There was never an inside and an outside group in the New Testament. Rather, there were those who opened to the Father's touch, and yes, even in the book of Acts, those who chose not to open to His touch. We see this reality in the apostles' handling of a situation in Acts 6:

> At this time while the disciples were increasing in number, a complaint arose on the part of the Hellenistic Jews against the Hebrews, because their widows were being overlooked in the daily serving of food. So the twelve summoned the congregation of the disciples and said, "It is not desirable for us to neglect the word of God in order to serve tables. Therefore, brethren, select from among you seven men of good reputation, full of the Spirit and of wisdom, whom we may put in charge of this task." (6:1–3)

Notice the criteria used here to define those whom the apostles would choose to wait tables: "Select from among you seven men of good reputation, full of the Spirit." It is quite obvious that if everyone had been "full of the Spirit," that requirement certainly wouldn't have been included as a prerequisite to serving in this situation. So we see that in the early years of the church, there were those who opened to the fullness of the Spirit's work and those who did not.

Clarifying the Purpose of the Baptism of the Holy Spirit

This filling of the Spirit is not necessarily the marker, or even *a* marker, for spiritual maturity, though many in the church have declared it to be. The filling with the Spirit is certainly to be desired and embraced to help empower one who desires to grow deeper with the Lord in touching and serving others, but it is in no way a guarantee that one will experience spiritual growth and maturity. Spiritual growth, also known as sanctification, develops in our day-to-day walk with God that includes time in prayer, in the Word and in worship that draws us near to the Father's heart.

The infilling of the Holy Spirit can in many ways enhance these activities, but there are many Spirit-filled believers who grow cold and unfruitful in their daily hunger and passion for Jesus. A cursory overview of the book of 1 Corinthians makes this very apparent. The church in Corinth moved in the power of the Spirit (see 1 Cor. 12–14). They operated in healing and in prophetic gifts, but they failed miserably in their day-to-day walk with God and with each other. There were divisions among them that allowed sin in the camp, and they had little or no conviction to deal with it:

> I exhort you, brethren, by the name of our Lord Jesus Christ, that you all agree and that there be no divisions among you, but that you be made complete in the same mind and in the same judgment. For I have been informed concerning you, my brethren, by Chloe's people, that there are quarrels among you. Now I mean this, that each one of you is saying, "I am of Paul," and "I of Apollos," and "I of Cephas," and "I of Christ." Has Christ been divided? Paul was not crucified for you, was he? Or were you baptized in the name of Paul? (1 Cor. 1:10–13)

> It is actually reported that there is immorality among you, and immorality of such a kind as does not exist even among the Gentiles, that someone has his father's wife. You have become arrogant and have not mourned instead, so that the one who had done this deed would be removed from your midst. (1 Cor. 5:1–2)

In light of this reality, it is crucial that we recognize and remain open to all that the Spirit brings to us. We must honor the Holy Spirit's multifaceted work of empowering the believer for works of ministry and of sanctifying, convicting and renewing us in our daily walk, and embrace all that He has set before us in His Word.

A Historical Look at the Spirit's Work

Historically speaking, the only renewal that the evangelical church has experienced has come through this "filling," or "baptism," that Jesus alone can give (see John 1:33). Godly men such as D. L. Moody, R. A. Torrey, Dr. Martyn Lloyd-Jones, Jonathan Edwards, Andrew Murray and John Wesley all experienced this power. R. A. Torrey, dean of Moody Bible Institute and of Biola College, said, "I sought earnestly that I might be baptized with the Holy Spirit. . . . The result was a transformed Christian life and a transformed ministry."

The baptism of the Holy Spirit is usually separate and distinct from the salvation experience, yet the two events may happen simultaneously at salvation. Jesus, on His last night before His crucifixion, declared to His disciples their need to cling to Him and to remain in relationship with Him at all times. This would certainly assume that salvation had taken place in them, as Jesus said, "You are already clean because of the word which I have spoken to you" (John 15:3).

Further, we see in John 20:22 that He imparted the Spirit to them: "He breathed on them, and said to them, 'Receive the Holy Spirit.'"

The word *receive* in the Greek text is in the aorist imperative. This tense never has a future meaning. Some would say that with His words above, Jesus was prophesying about Acts chapter 2, the event of Pentecost, but that is impossible. Jesus was not speaking to His disciples about some experience yet to come; He was sealing their salvation with the Holy Spirit (see Eph. 1:13 below). This is very important to those who have been taught that there is no "second experience" of Holy Spirit baptism after salvation, when in fact biblically there is.

You see, Jesus later told these same men who had already received the Holy Spirit from Him personally to tarry until they were *baptized* with the Holy Spirit (see Acts 1:4–5), which would happen at Pentecost. But in John 20:22 Jesus was declaring the salvation of His disciples and the *sealing* work of the Holy Spirit, described by Paul in Ephesians:

> In Him, you also, after listening to the message of truth, the gospel of your salvation—having also believed, you were sealed in Him with the Holy Spirit of promise. (1:13)

This sealing of the Spirit in the disciples took place before Pentecost in the Upper Room, according to John 20:22, and the baptizing power came later at Pentecost: "John baptized with water, but you will be baptized with the Holy Spirit not many days from now" (Acts 1:5).

It is at Pentecost that we can see the purpose of this baptism clearly defined:

> When they had come together, they were asking Him, saying, "Lord, is it at this time You are restoring the kingdom to Israel?" He said to them, "It is not for you to know times or epochs which the Fat-

her has fixed by His own authority; but you will receive power when the Holy Spirit has come upon you; and you shall be My witnesses both in Jerusalem, and in all Judea and Samaria, and even to the remotest part of the earth." (Acts 1:6–8)

The Defining Purpose of the Spirit's Baptism or Filling

Acts 1:8 sets the perimeters and purpose of this impartation of the Spirit:

> You will receive power when the Holy Spirit has come upon you; and you shall be My witnesses both in Jerusalem, and in all Judea and Samaria, and even to the remotest part of the earth.

The empowering work of the Spirit is primarily intended to be used in outreach, in touching and healing others in Jesus' name. Repeatedly in the book of Acts, we find believers experiencing and embracing this empowering for ministry; thus, we believe that the baptism of the Holy Spirit ought to be embraced today if we are to do Christ's ministry effectively:

> When the apostles in Jerusalem heard that Samaria had received the word of God, they sent them Peter and John, who came down and prayed for them, that they might receive the Holy Spirit. For He had not yet fallen upon any of them; they had simply been baptized in the name of the Lord Jesus. Then they began laying their hands on them, and they were receiving the Holy Spirit. (Acts 8:14–17)

Ananias departed and entered the house, and after laying his hands on him said, "Brother Saul, the Lord Jesus, who appeared to you on the road by which you were coming, has sent me so that you may regain your sight, and be filled with the Holy Spirit." (9:17)

While Peter was still speaking these words, the Holy Spirit fell upon all those who were listening to the message. All the circumcised believers who came with Peter were amazed, because the gift of the Holy Spirit had been poured out on the Gentiles also. For they were hearing them speaking with tongues and exalting God. Then Peter answered, "Surely no one can refuse the water for these to be baptized who have received the Holy Spirit just as we did, can he?"And he ordered them to be baptized in the name of Jesus Christ. Then they asked him to stay on for a few days. (10:44–48)

And it happened that while Apollos was at Corinth, Paul passed through the upper country and came to Ephesus, and found some disciples. He said to them, "Did you receive the Holy Spirit when you believed?" And they said to him, "No, we have not even heard whether there is a Holy Spirit." And he said, "Into what then were you baptized?" And they said, "Into John's baptism." Paul said, "John baptized with the baptism of repentance, telling the people to believe in Him who was coming after him, that is, in Jesus." When they heard this, they were baptized in the name of the Lord Jesus. And when Paul had laid his hands upon them, the Holy Spirit came on them, and they began speaking with tongues and prophesying. There were in all about twelve men. (19:1–7)

Spirit-Filled Living as a Daily Lifestyle

This baptism, or filling, should be an ongoing part of the Christian life, not just a one-time experience. For any of us to be effective for Jesus, we need His power to do His work, and we need it every day. We need to be refilled and renewed in order to remain fresh, passionate and vibrant for Jesus. This is the example that we see in Peter's life. We are told in the book of Acts that Peter was touched, baptized and filled no less than three times. Peter was with the disciples in the Upper Room and filled with the Spirit at that time (see Acts 2:1, 4), yet in Acts 4:8 and also in 4:31, we are told that he received a fresh filling of the Spirit:

> Then Peter, having been filled with the Holy Spirit, said unto them: "Rulers of the people, and elders of Israel, if we to-day are examined concerning the good deed to the ailing man, by whom he hath been saved, be it known to all of you, and to all the people of Israel, that in the name of Jesus Christ of Nazareth, whom ye did crucify, whom God did raise out of the dead, in Him hath this one stood by before you whole." (4:8–10, YLT)

> And they having prayed, the place was shaken in which they were gathered together, and they were all filled with the Holy Spirit, and were speaking the word of God with freedom, and of the multitude of those who did believe the heart and the soul was one, and not one was saying that anything of the

things he had was his own, but all things were to them in common. (4:31–32, YLT)

Once we have experienced the ministry of the Spirit in our lives, it becomes a daily activity of Spirit-filled believers to continue to invite the Holy Spirit's touch in our lives and to remain open to His work.

Receiving the Baptism of the Spirit

Some desire the work of the Spirit for the wrong reasons. They have seen their friends touched, they have heard about certain sign gifts being manifested and desire to experience those gifts, or they are simply looking for a new experience with God. The baptism of the Spirit certainly includes the miraculous touch of Jesus, but God doesn't touch us so that we can be touched—He touches us so that we can touch others.

God gives the Holy Spirit to those who seek His touch in their lives and ministries, and His Word is clear that He gives to those who ask and keep asking—to those who seek Jesus, not His gifts or power:

> I say to you, ask, and it will be given to you; seek, and you will find; knock, and it will be opened to you. For everyone who asks, receives; and he who seeks, finds; and to him who knocks, it shall be opened. Now suppose one of you fathers is asked by his son for a fish; he will not give him a snake instead of a fish, will he? Or if he is asked for an egg, he will not give him a scorpion will he? If you then, being evil, know how to give good gifts to your children, how much more will your heavenly Father give the Holy Spirit to those who ask Him? (Luke 11:9–13)

Don't be discouraged if the first time you open to the Holy Spirit's touch, you don't sense Him moving in you. Pursue Him with all your heart, and you will, according to His promise, find Him. He will meet you. You may seek Him in private, in a class or at a service. We encourage you to come to those who will pray with you at the altar at church, to those on the church ministry team or to other Spirit-filled believers and ask them to lay hands on you and invite the Holy Spirit's touch as you open to Him.

Once the Spirit has touched you, you should expect that the baptism of the Holy Spirit will be followed by a release of charismata, or sign gifts. This may or may not include speaking in tongues, but surely we should expect miraculous things to follow the baptism as they did in the New Testament:

> To each one is given the manifestation of the Spirit for the common good. For to one is given the word of wisdom through the Spirit, and to another the word of knowledge according to the same Spirit; to another faith by the same Spirit, and to another gifts of healing by the one Spirit, and to another the effecting of miracles, and to another prophecy, and to another the distinguishing of spirits, to another various kinds of tongues, and to another the interpretation of tongues. But one and the same Spirit works all these things, distributing to each one individually just as He wills. (1 Cor. 12:7–11)

These gifts may include power to impart physical healing or emotional healing, supernatural prophetic insight or the ability to discern deeply in the spiritual realm as well as the gift of a prayer language, often known as the gift of tongues. Each of these gifts is found throughout the New Testament.

Before We Close

We believe at Water of Life that all gifts should be used in an orderly and biblical fashion, according to the guidelines found in 1 Corinthians 14:26–33. It should be said that we are aware that when people exercise any gift from God, there will be times that they misuse those gifts. Our knowing this is neither an excuse nor a license for people to abuse the gifts, but that they will is a spiritual reality, and it is the reason that our pastors are trained to help keep biblical boundaries around the use of these supernatural gifts. It is our job as elders and pastors to kindly give instruction in these practices. Our goal is to give order to the use of gifts, not to shut them down because some would abuse them.

Appendix A: Spiritual Gifts

Prophecy

A. We believe in the New Testament's use of prophecy as outlined in 1 Corinthians 12, 13 and 14. This would include the public use of prophecy as outlined in 1 Corinthians 14:26–33 and the more private ministry of the gift of knowledge, or the "word of wisdom" or "word of knowledge," found in 1 Corinthians 12:8: "For to one is given the word of wisdom through the Spirit, and to another the word of knowledge according to the same Spirit."

B. We believe that the gift of prophecy is used for edification, exhortation and consolation as is taught in 1 Corinthians 14:3—in other words, to build up, encourage and console. It must be used within the biblical guidelines of 1 Corinthians 12, 13 and 14. This includes being kind, gentle and loving when exercising the gift of prophecy.

C. We believe that our prophetic words must not trap others into a course of action—for example, "God says that you must do this or that." Rather, we must remain open to the possibility of at least partial error: "I think God may be saying this to you—does that make any sense?" "For we know in part and we prophesy in part" (1 Cor. 13:9).

D. We believe that the gift of prophecy ought to be used to confirm what God is doing in you already. If a word given to you does not do this, put it on the shelf for later reference, and don't try to be self-fulfilling or to live under what was spoken to you by another person. Remember that New Testament believers (including you) were given the Holy Spirit and the Bible to guide us daily in all we do.

E. We believe that only those whose lives and gifting we know personally ought to exercise the gift of prophecy in a public assembly. We would in no way seek to hinder the flow of the Spirit of God by telling a person not to prophesy. However, if a person is new to this assembly or unsure that what he feels led to speak is from God, that individual should take the word to a pastor or elder so that the leadership can decide a course of action at that time.

Prayer for Healing

A. We believe in praying for healing of the sick and of the emotionally and spiritually wounded: "Is anyone among you sick? Let him call for the elders of the church, and let them pray over him, anointing him with oil in the name of the Lord" (James 5:14, ESV).

B. We believe that laying on of hands is often appropriate during prayer: "He has seen in a vision a man named Ananias come in and lay his hands on him, so that he might regain his sight" (Acts 9:12).

C. We believe that concerted, pointed prayer for freedom, or deliverance, from demonic spirits is biblical and often appropriate, but we ask that this always be overseen by a trained leader or pastor and that it be done with great sensitivity both to the Holy Spirit and to the person involved.

The Gift of Tongues

We believe that there are three means of expression for this gift's use:

1. Personal prayer in which the person using the gift of tongues is built up as he prays.

> One who speaks in a tongue does not speak to men,

> but to God; for no one understands, but in his spirit he speaks mysteries. But one who prophesies speaks to men for edification and exhortation and consolation. One who speaks in a tongue edifies himself; but one who prophesies edifies the church. (1 Cor. 14:2–4)

> If I pray in a tongue, my spirit prays, but my mind is unfruitful. What is the outcome then? I will pray with the spirit and I will pray with the mind also; I will sing with the spirit and I will sing with the mind also. (1 Cor. 14:14–15)

2. The public use of the gift of tongues. This use must always be followed by an interpretation.

> But now, brethren, if I come to you speaking in tongues, what will I profit you unless I speak to you either by way of revelation or of knowledge or of prophesy or of teaching? (1 Cor. 14:6)

> What is the outcome then, brethren? When you assemble, each one has a psalm, has a teaching, has a revelation, has a tongue, has an interpretation. Let all things be done for edification. If anyone speaks in a tongue, it should be by two or at the most three, and each in turn, and one must interpret; but if there is no interpreter, let him keep silent in the church; and let him speak to himself and to God. (1 Cor. 14:26–28)

3. The gift of tongues when used to "sing with the spirit."

> What is the outcome then? I will pray with the spirit and I will pray with the mind also; I will sing with the spirit and I will sing with the mind also. (1 Cor. 14:15)

> Be careful how you walk, not as unwise men but as wise, making the most of your time, because the days are evil. So then do not be foolish, but understand what the will of the Lord is. And do not get drunk with wine, for that is dissipation, but be filled with the Spirit, speaking to one another in psalms and hymns and spiritual songs, singing and making melody with your heart to the Lord; always giving thanks for all things in the name of our Lord Jesus Christ to God, even the Father. (Eph. 5:15–20)

Recommended Reading

We recommend several books for further clarification on this issue. We believe that these books provide a godly, biblical and evangelical perspective on both the gifts and the baptism of the Holy Spirit:

> The book of Acts in the New Testament
> *The Beauty of Spiritual Language* by Jack Hayford
> *Joy Unspeakable* by Dr. Martyn Lloyd-Jones
> *Secret Power* by Dwight L. Moody
> *Divine Healing* by Andrew Murray
> *The Spirit of Christ* by Andrew Murray
> *The Person and Work of the Holy Spirit* by R. A. Torrey

The Ministry and Gift of Prophecy

Prophecy is often found to be mysterious, difficult, a bit strange and, at best, non-useful to most practical people. The truth is that God, throughout the ages, has used prophecy to build a bridge to men and women that allows them to glimpse not only Him but His workings with people.

Beginning in the Old Testament, prophecy and the prophets who delivered it held a valuable and esteemed place in all the work God did. In fact, a major portion of the Old Testament includes books named after prophets. We divide these books into two groups: the major prophets and the minor prophets. The major prophets include Isaiah, Jeremiah, Lamentations, Ezekiel and Daniel, while the minor prophets make up the last twelve books of the Old Testament: Hosea, Joel, Amos, Obadiah, Jonah, Micah, Nahum, Habakkuk, Zephaniah, Haggai, Zechariah and Malachi. The significance of these prophetic books is clear in the New Testament, as Jesus stated:

> These are My words which I spoke to you while I was still with you, that all things which are written about Me in the Law of Moses and the Prophets and the Psalms must be fulfilled. (Luke 24:44)

Clarifying Old Testament Prophecy

Often we view the prophetic books as historical Old Testament stuff that is rarely applicable today. This is a major mistake on our part.

The Old Testament prophets did two things that make them important to us today. First, they foretold the future. Some of the events they prophesied have come to pass, while some have yet to unfold and which may actually take place in our lifetime. Most of us, if challenged, would agree that prophecy is what we've just defined: foretelling the future. And as we just saw, this is part of prophecy, but only a portion.

Much of the ministry of both Old and New Testament prophecy and prophetic ministry, however, has less to do with the future and more to do with the present. This second aspect of prophecy is forth-telling, not foretelling. Forth-telling may actually impact each of us in greater ways than the more widely understood aspect of foretelling. It is declaring the present, clarifying the present—helping us to get a grasp on what God is up to in the here and now.

We find both of these facets of prophecy throughout prophetic ministry in the Bible.

Old Testament Prophets and Prophecy

In the Old Testament, prophecy and prophets operated with two very clear distinguishing features. First, God used both the function of prophecy and the office of prophet to communicate His will, direction and correction to Israel. Prophecy was the mouth of God in the Old Testament. Second, because of the critical role that prophecy held in directing God's people, perfection in its delivery was the standard. A prophet had to be 100 percent accurate and true. False prophets were not tolerated (see Deut. 18:20–22) and were condemned to death for betraying God and leading people astray.

This all changed at Pentecost when the Holy Spirit was given to the church. Now God's voice and the written Word would lead the New Testament church, and prophecy would only be used to confirm what God had spoken. With this in mind, it is critical for us to view prophecy and the office of prophet with clarity as we differentiate the roles and functions of this ministry in both the Old and New Testaments.

The Old Testament is full of prophets and prophetic instances. Abraham is called a prophet in Genesis 20:7, Aaron likewise in Exodus 7:1; their sister Miriam is called a prophetess in Exodus 15:20, and Deborah too was called a prophetess in Judges 4:4. With a cursory glance at the Pentateuch (the first five books of the Old Testament) and the historical books (the twelve books following the Pentateuch), we can see that prophetic ministry permeates the Old Testament.

Looking first at Moses, we see the seventy elders whom Moses had gathered prophesying in Numbers 11: "When the Spirit rested upon them, they prophesied. But they did not do it again" (11:25). It is worth noting that two men, Eldad and Medad, who were not in the meeting with Moses and the seventy elders but were instead back in the camp, also prophesied (see 11:26). Clearly God's Spirit was moving, and Moses declared such in verses 28–29 when he was challenged about these two who had not been in the meeting prophesying:

> Then Joshua the son of Nun, the attendant of Moses from his youth, said, "Moses, my lord, restrain them." But Moses said to him, "Are you jealous for my sake? Would that all the Lord's people were prophets, that the LORD would put His Spirit upon them!"

The seventy elders were never used again by the Spirit for prophetic ministry, according to the text. They prophesied, but they were not prophets. It is also evident that Moses loved what the Spirit was doing and fully embraced this prophetic moment, declaring that he wished "all the Lord's people were prophets."

Another telling prophetic incident captured in the Old Testament included a young King Saul. Shortly after being anointed as king by the prophet Samuel, Saul was told that God would move on him to transform him while he was in the act of prophesying:

> You will meet a group of prophets coming down from the high place with harp, tambourine, flute, and a lyre before them, and they will be prophesying. Then the Spirit of the LORD will come upon you mightily, and you shall prophesy with them and be changed into another man. (1 Sam. 10:5–6)

This isn't the only time Saul prophesied (see 1 Sam. 19:20–24), yet he was a king and was never recognized as a prophet. David also functioned as a king who prophesied throughout the Psalms:

> Now these are the last words of David. David the son of Jesse declares, the man who was raised on high declares, the anointed of the God of Jacob, and the sweet psalmist of Israel, "The Spirit of the LORD spoke by me, and His word was on my tongue." (2 Sam. 23:1–2)

God declared Moses a prophet while outlining the Old Testament prophetic guidelines. Deuteronomy 18:18–22 states,

> "I will raise up a prophet from among their countrymen like you, and I will put My words in his mouth, and he shall speak to them all that I command him. It shall come about that whoever will not listen to My words which he shall speak in My name, I Myself will require it of him. But the prophet who speaks a word presumptuously in My name which I have not commanded him to speak, or which he speaks in the name of other gods, that prophet shall die." You may say in your heart, "How will we know the word which the LORD has not

spoken?" When a prophet speaks in the name of the LORD, if the thing does not come about or come true, that is the thing which the LORD has not spoken. The prophet has spoken it presumptuously; you shall not be afraid of him.

Clearly the prophet in the Old Testament reported directly to God. Prophets were God's mouthpiece, and as such, there was no room for them to err or to move falsely in His name, lest they fall under the penalty of death.

Office of Prophet

It is important to differentiate between the Old Testament prophets and those whom the Holy Spirit came upon who prophesied. This is the difference between the office of prophet and a person who prophesies. As a little boy, Samuel occupied the office of prophet, and his words were the words of the Lord:

> Thus Samuel grew and the LORD was with him and let none of his words fail. All Israel from Dan even to Beersheba knew that Samuel was confirmed as a prophet of the LORD. (1 Sam. 3:19–20)

Samuel's life was given to the office of prophet. His was a life call from God, not a moment of prophetic anointing. He filled an office that held high esteem in Israel, operating alongside the king and the priest as rulers over the nation. Prophets were the medium for God's voice, and it was God and God alone who could raise them up. Amos 3:7 declares such: "The Lord GOD does nothing without revealing his secret to his servants the prophets" (ESV).

The prophet directed kings and corrected Israel, as we see in the ministries of Isaiah, Zechariah, Ezekiel and many others. This office of prophet, along with that of priest and king, was God's primary means for leading and ministering to Israel, God's people in the Old Testament. The functions of this office changed dramatically at Pentecost. Though we find the office of prophet functioning in the New Testament (see Eph. 4:11), we do not find the prophet functioning with the same authority or accountability as in the Old Testament model.

New Testament Prophecy

The great gift of the New Testament was the outpouring of the Holy Spirit onto all God's people. We no longer need a priest to make sacrifices for us, since Jesus has atoned for our sins (see Heb. 7:21) and, in fact, as we are all now part of the priesthood of believers:

> But you are a chosen race, a royal priesthood, a holy nation, a people for God's own possession, so that you may proclaim the excellencies of Him who has called you out of darkness into His marvelous light. (1 Pet. 2:9)

Likewise, we no longer need the prophet to declare the word of the Lord to us, as we all now have God's Spirit working in us and revealing the Father to us. Jesus made this clear:

> I will ask the Father, and He will give you another Helper, that He may be with you forever; that is the Spirit of truth, whom the world cannot receive, because it does not see Him or know Him, but you know Him because He abides with you and will be in you. . . . These things I have spoken to you while abiding with you. But the Helper, the Holy Spirit, whom the Father will send in My name, He will

teach you all things, and bring to your remembrance all that I said to you. (John 14:16–17, 25–26)

So New Testament prophetic gifting and the office of prophet remain, but with an entirely different role and function than they had in the Old Testament. This distinction is made clear when Paul outlines prophetic ministry and the gifts of the Holy Spirit in 1 Corinthians chapters 12, 13 and 14. In 1 Corinthians 13:8–9 Paul declares,

> Love never fails; but if there are gifts of prophecy, they will be done away; if there are tongues, they will cease; if there is knowledge, it will be done away. For we know in part and we prophesy in part.

"For we know in part and we prophesy in part"—unlike in the Old Testament, there is implied here a grace to fail. For prophecy, though very useful, is no longer the mouthpiece of God. God's Spirit and His Word now take that role. New Testament prophecy is still given, according to 1 Corinthians 14:3, but one who prophesies speaks "to men for edification and exhortation and consolation." New Testament prophetic gifting encourages and builds up the church, confirming what the Spirit is saying.

The distinguishing feature of New Testament prophecy is that it is now deemed a spiritual gift imparted by the Holy Spirit (see Rom. 12:6; 1 Cor. 12:10). This means that all now have the potential to prophesy, according to 1 Corinthians 14:24, and that we should all "desire earnestly spiritual gifts, but especially that [we] may prophesy" (1 Cor. 14:1). This is a fulfillment of the prophet Joel's words quoted in Acts 2:17–18:

> "And it shall be in the last days," God says, "that I will pour forth of My Spirit on all mankind; and

your sons and your daughters shall prophesy, and your young men shall see visions, and your old men shall dream dreams; even on My bondslaves, both men and women, I will in those days pour forth of My Spirit and they shall prophesy."

New Testament Gift and Office of Prophet

The distinction between the office of prophet and the gift of prophecy is also evident, though blurred, in the New Testament. We are certain that there were prophets in the New Testament, as Acts 11:27–28 details:

> Now at this time some prophets came down from Jerusalem to Antioch. One of them named Agabus stood up and began to indicate by the Spirit that there would certainly be a great famine all over the world. And this took place in the reign of Claudius.

First Corinthians 12:28 also states that "God has appointed in the church, first apostles, second prophets." Acts mentions prophets numerous times (see Acts 15:32; 21:9–10), but it is clear that the office of prophet took on a vastly different role in the early church than it held in Old Testament times.

Ephesians 2:20 states that prophets helped to establish the church, which is "built on the foundation of the apostles and prophets." G. W. H. Lamp, in his work *Christ and Spirit in the New Testament*, states,

> Within the New Testament period there seems to have been a definite, though to us obscure, distinction between occasional prophesying by "ordinary"

church members, on the one hand, and the exercise of a ministry by "specialist" prophets on the other.

In fact, the line between those who prophesy and those who are called prophets is blurred quite often (see 1 Cor. 14:31–32). For Paul prophecy is revelation. It is a word or insight from God. A prophecy is not a prepared message, though prophetic revelation may come forth in a sermon. Spontaneity marks this divine gift and its work. It is certainly seen as valuable and supernatural, as Paul lists prophecy just after miracles in the 1 Corinthians 12:10 gift list. But it is clear that this spontaneous word from the Lord does not hold the same value as the written Scriptures do. As we stated earlier, in prophecy God now works within the limits of our humanness, meaning that we know in part and prophesy in part, which leaves room for human error.

The purpose of the gift of prophecy in the New Testament is outlined in its entirety in 1 Corinthians 14:3: "But one who prophesies speaks to men for edification and exhortation and consolation."

Edification (*oikodome*) is actually two words combined that mean "to build the house": *oikos*, meaning "house," and *doma/demo*, "to build." These words tell us that prophecy is a tool that God uses to build us up, to encourage us and to strengthen us.

The second purpose of prophecy, exhortation, comes from the word *paraklesis*. *Para* means "to come alongside," and *kaleo* means "to call." *Exhortation* means "to come near and comfort" or "to call to," as if to summon a person to move ahead in a direction.

Finally, Paul used the word *consolation* (*paramuthia*), which means "to persuade" or "to console"—in other words, to help people hear what God is doing so that they can rest in His action and trust Him. So prophecy is intended to build us, move us, comfort us and console us.

Ephesians 4:11–12 identifies the New Testament office of prophet, which is filled by those gifted with a particular accuracy of prophecy, as vital to the building up of the body of Christ:

> He gave some as apostles, and some as prophets, and some as evangelists, and some as pastors and teachers, for the equipping of the saints for the work of service, to the building up of the body of Christ.

Without these five ministries functioning in the local church, the saints often fail to become all that God has intended them to be. So the New Testament office of prophet continues to hold a vital, though less defining, role in the church than it did in the Old Testament.

Processing Prophetic Words

Each of these prophetic processes is meant to confirm what the Spirit has already said or will say to an individual. Prophecies are not in and of themselves "the word of the Lord," as they were in the Old Testament. Many believers err here, revamping their whole life around a word they received from someone. The wisest thing we can do is to take all prophetic words spoken to us and put them on the shelf of our life. We should pray over them, asking the Spirit to speak to us, and test the prophecies in the Word.

In the New Testament we are to direct our lives by the written Word and by the Holy Spirit, using prophecy to clarify and confirm what the Spirit is saying to us. It is not an accident that the gift of discernment is always found listed nearby the gift of prophecy (see 1 Cor. 12:10; 14:29; 1 Thess. 5:20–21; 1 John 4:1).

Each word and thought that we receive should be prayerfully tested and discerned. Prophecy contains great potential to touch and change lives, but it also, by its high-powered nature, contains the ability to wound and hurt if it is not handled correctly. True prophecy will never violate Scripture or the heart of the Father. It is harmonious with the Word and with the nature of God. True prophetic ministry will build up, not tear down; it will bear witness with others and will glorify God, not man.

Prophecy can also be used by the Spirit to bring unbelievers to Jesus. Though prophecy is primarily a gift for believers, it can and often does bring a conviction to unbelievers (see 1 Cor. 14:22). This conviction can open people up to meet and experience the great hope and healing that God has for them:

> If all prophesy, and an unbeliever or an ungifted man enters, he is convicted by all, he is called to account by all; the secrets of his heart are disclosed; and so he will fall on his face and worship God, declaring that God is certainly among you. (1 Cor. 14:24–25)

In conclusion, all prophecy should bring life. We should hunger to prophesy (see 1 Cor. 14:1). Prophecy should be orderly (see 1 Cor. 14:29–31). It should be discerned and judged freely and openly, and it should not be confusing but clarifying (see 1 Cor. 14:32–33). In the end it should bring life from the heart of God.

Appendix B: Functioning in the Gift of Prophecy

Prophecy

The gift of prophecy is the special ability to receive and communicate an immediate message of God to His people through a divinely anointed utterance.

What Is Prophecy?

Prophecy is speaking God's heart, mind and purpose by the inspiration of the Holy Spirit. This speaking incorporates the revelatory and prophetic things of the Spirit that are resident in the one speaking. It is done primarily to build up, encourage, comfort and communicate a fuller counsel of God to His people. Since we are all imperfect vessels, it is important to have all prophecy brought into the light and judged.

The Primary Purpose of Prophecy

"But one who prophesies speaks to men for edification and exhortation and consolation" (1 Cor. 14:3).

Who May Prophesy?

"For you can all prophesy in turn so that everyone may be instructed and encouraged" (1 Cor. 14:31, NIV).

Prophetic Protocol

The following guidelines are set up to protect the one giving the prophecy, anyone listening to the prophecy and the prophetic ministry itself. "Everything should be done in a fitting and orderly way" (1 Cor. 14:40, NIV).

No dates. Jesus Himself gave no specific dates regarding His return.

No mates. We are not to tell a person whom they should marry, divorce, etc.

No deaths or births. Telling a person of a coming baby or an impending death can bring heartache and confusion.

No correction or specific direction. Correction and specific direction should come from those to whom God has given a place of authority, covering and accountability over a person's life.

"Thus saith the Lord." We prefer that prophetic words be prefaced with "I sense," "I see," "I believe that the Lord is saying," etc. *This leaves room for error on the part of both the one giving the word and the one receiving it.* "We know in part and we prophesy in part" (1 Cor. 13:9).

Prophecy should be judged. First, when receiving a prophetic word from someone, it should be judged against the "more sure word of prophecy" (2 Pet. 1:19, KJV)—the Bible. Let two or three prophets speak, and let those believers who hear it judge (see 1 Cor. 14:29). All new information must be consistent with the existing, inerrant Word of God. Second, any prophecy we receive should bear witness with our inner witness, causing us to feel built up, encouraged and comforted. We should not receive prophecy from someone who resists having the prophecy judged by church leaders (see 1 Cor. 14:29). When we receive a personal prophecy, it is a good idea to write it down or record it. This will serve to judge the prophecy as well as to bless those who receive the word.

The Ministry and Gifts of Biblical Healing

When most of us get sick, the first thought we have is to call a doctor. And that is certainly a legitimate response. But what if we actually believed that God was for us and that He was compassionate and caring (He actually is much more caring than we are) and we stopped and asked for His healing touch in prayer? Sounds a bit unusual in this day and age of the rational scientific mind, but the truth is that when we are sick or hurt and the doctors can't help us, God is the first one most of us turn to. Rarely would we identify this as asking for divine healing, but it certainly is.

Divine healing is an issue that lies at the heart of Christianity. If we were talking about theology, we would call divine healing a core issue, because it relates to God's love for people and His desire to both restore and forgive. All salvation is predicated on God's hungering passion to rectify the destruction that sin has wrought in us spiritually, emotionally and physically. The deepest sickness we experience in this life is the sickness of sin, and the truth is, all other sickness flows out of this debilitating disease. Fortunately, God is a forgiving, kind and compassionate Father who has dealt with the consequences of sin and the damage it does to so many areas of our lives. Healing in all its forms, whether physical, emotional or spiritual, is a natural demonstration of God's compassion toward the people He created and loves. Healing lies at the heart of God's salvation message for mankind.

Jesus' Healing Ministry

Jesus' healing ministry is actually a wonderful picture of the Father's heart for people. We see the compassion of God when Jesus touched and healed "many who were ill with various diseases" (Mark 1:34). And the good news is, physical healing didn't end with Jesus' ministry; in fact, it was just beginning. Jesus made that clear when He declared that the kingdom of God was at hand and then directed the seventy-two to "heal the sick . . . and say to them, 'The kingdom of God has come near to you'" (Luke 10:9, ESV). Later He declared that His people would "place their hands on sick people, and they [would] get well" (Mark 16:18, NIV), thus ensuring that healing ministry would become a vital aspect of His coming church.

The reality of these and other New Testament declarations make it clear that healing is foundational to the kingdom of God. Many of us aren't familiar with the term "the kingdom of God," but it was the key phrase that Jesus used when describing the work He was doing on Earth. The kingdom of God is literally the place where God rules and reigns—the King's domain, His realm of dominion over evil and Satan. Jesus used healing to demonstrate His authority over sickness and His desire to restore and renew those who have been damaged by sin. Each of us who has surrendered to God is actually part of this kingdom. As such, we enjoy a bit of the fruit of the kingdom now, like healing ministry, but we are all keenly aware that we have yet to see God's kingdom in all the fullness of which the book of Revelation speaks.

Sickness and Judgment in the Old Testament

One of the confusing aspects of healing ministry is the distinct difference in how the Old and New Testaments portray God in physical healing. Because of this many people would argue that divine healing is not always what God has in mind or desires to do. They would accurately state that the Old Testament is full of pictures of God using sickness and disease to discipline and bring judgment on His people, Israel. Exodus 15:26 makes this point rather boldly:

> If you will give earnest heed to the voice of the LORD your God, and do what is right in His sight, and give ear to His commandments, and keep all His statutes, I will put none of the diseases on you which I have put on the Egyptians; for I, the LORD, am your healer.

It is clear throughout the Old Testament that Israel's physical health, or lack thereof, was always a reflection of their spiritual wellbeing and obedience. But it is also quite obvious that God is a healer, as it is He who added, "For I, the LORD, am your healer." As commentators Keil and Delitzsch aptly state, "All that is clear and undoubted is . . . Jehovah made Himself known to the people of Israel as their Physician." Also, God was declared such by His Old Testament name of Jehovah-Rapha, which the New International Version translates, "I am the LORD, who heals you" (Exod. 15:26).

So did God heal in the Old Testament? The answer is an unequivocal yes (see Hezekiah's healing in 2 Kings 20:1–11). Did He also use sickness to discipline His people? The answer is yes. In the Old Testament Israel's relationship with God was always straining under the law. It was "keep the guidelines and get life; walk away and get an immediate response both physically and spiritually." Fortunately for us, we live in the age of grace. Does God still hate sin and the consequences it brings to people? Yes! But the consequences of sin are tempered by the cross and the sacrifice of Jesus' own life. Because of this we experience much more liberty to enter into a deeper and more life-giving relationship with Him than did God's people in the Old Testament.

Reconciling the Old and New Testament Views of Sin and Sickness

How do we reconcile the pictures between the Old Testament and the New Testament? First and foremost, it is essential for us to understand that the New Testament doesn't conflict with the Old Testament; rather, it clarifies it. When Jesus declared early in His ministry that the kingdom of God was near (see Mark 1:15), He immediately followed this pronouncement by healing the sick and casting out demons. Later, when He healed a demonized man, He told the Pharisees, "If I cast out demons by the Spirit of God, then the kingdom of God has come upon you" (Matt. 12:28).

These and other demonstrations and declarations by Jesus show us that the New Testament's focus is clearly on Satan's ability to derail God's people rather than on the weakness and sinfulness of the people. Jesus' statements that wholeness is related to His kingdom bring to the forefront the fact that Satan has a role in people's sin, sickness, poverty and oppression and help immensely to clear up the role that disease and judgment have in relationship to healing and obedience.

That is not to say that some sickness isn't caused by disobedience and sin, but not all sickness is a result of personal sin. Jesus corrects His disciples' Old Testament perspective that regularly connected sickness and disease with the judgment of God. In John 9:1–3 He is questioned by His disciples about a blind man that He heals:

> As He passed by, He saw a man blind from birth. And His disciples asked Him, "Rabbi, who sinned, this man or his parents, that he would be born blind?" Jesus answered, "It was neither that this man sinned, nor his parents; but it was so that the works of God might be displayed in him."

John Wimber makes this point when he aptly states in his book, *Power Healing,*

> The rule of the New Testament is that the righteous suffer the majority of all recorded satanic attacks. . . . Jesus Himself was an innocent sufferer, all of His disciples (except John) died violently, and the entire book of 1 Peter is about suffering for Christ.

The Foundation for All Biblical Healing

A close look at the prophetic picture of Jesus in Isaiah 53 will help to bring God's heart and will into focus for us, since it addresses both sin and the impact of salvation on people:

> Who has believed our message? And to whom has the arm of the LORD been revealed? For He grew up before Him like a tender shoot, and like a root out of parched ground; He has no stately form or majesty that we should look upon Him, nor appearance that we should be attracted to Him. He was despised and forsaken of men, a man of sorrows and acquainted with grief; and like one from whom men hide their face He was despised, and we did not esteem Him.
>
> Surely our griefs He Himself bore, and our sorrows He carried; yet we ourselves esteemed Him stricken, smitten of God, and afflicted. But He was pierced through for our transgressions, He was crushed for our iniquities; the chastening for our well-being fell upon Him, and by His scourging we are healed. All of us like sheep have gone astray, each of us has turned to his own way; but the LORD has caused the iniquity of us all to fall on Him. (Isa. 53:1–6)

Isaiah 53:1–6 is crucial for a biblical understanding of healing, because it addresses the atonement of Christ, which is the fundamental doctrine of the Bible. The atonement is the foundation for all other doctrines, including healing ministry. The word *atonement* means "to make as one," which is what God set out to do between us and Him when sin estranged men and women from Himself. Sin cuts off our relationship with God (see Rom. 3:23), and there is nothing we can do to fix that, according to Romans 3:20. But the atonement, Jesus' death on the cross, did what we could not do for ourselves. He paid the price of our sins and atoned for them; thus, the atonement is the healing that we all need. "He made Him who knew no sin to be sin on our behalf, so that we might become the righteousness of God in Him" (2 Cor. 5:21).

The question often raised is, "What did Jesus' death on the cross actually accomplish?" Was this atonement, this forgiveness of sins, a promise of perfect health? Jesus' death on the cross took away our sins, but did it also remove all our disease?

Isaiah 53:4 states, "Surely our griefs He Himself bore, and our sorrows He carried." These two words, *griefs* and *sorrows*, are crucial to understanding what Jesus accomplished on the cross. He bore both our griefs and our sorrows and took them to the cross, putting them under His blood. What are our griefs and sorrows?

The Hebrew word used for *griefs* in Isaiah 53:4 is *choli*. This word is used twenty-two times in the Old Testament, but only twice, in Isaiah 53:3–4, is it translated "grief" or "griefs"—every other time it is translated "sickness," "illness" or "affliction."

The second word, *sorrows*, is *makob*, and its root word *kaab*, as you might have guessed, also has dual meanings and can be translated as such. The *Theological Wordbook of the Old Testament* notes that of the sixteen times this word is used, twelve of them denote mental anguish or sorrow, while four of them deal with physical issues.

Even though only four usages of *kaab* refer to physical pain, however, it is impossible to separate the mental and physical anguish from the meaning of this word. A case in point would be in Exodus 3:7, where God's compassion for His people's affliction in their slavery is expressed. Surely they were suffering physical pain, but their total situation was cause for anguish as well.

My point is quite simple: these words describe sin's impact as both physical and mental, which means that Jesus carried our griefs and sorrows as well as our sickness and pain to the cross. This position is clearly supported in the New Testament when Matthew references Isaiah 53:4 in his discussion of Jesus healing Peter's mother-in-law and all those brought to Him who were ill:

> When Jesus came into Peter's home, He saw his mother-in-law lying sick in bed with a fever. He touched her hand, and the fever left her; and she got up and waited on Him. When evening came, they brought to Him many who were demon-possessed; and He cast out the spirits with a word, and healed all who were ill. This was to fulfill what was spoken through Isaiah the prophet: "He Himself took our infirmities and carried away our diseases." (Matt. 8:14–17)

The Atonement and Healing

This text leaves no doubt that the atonement can and does include physical healing. R. A. Torrey says of this passage,

> It is often said that this verse teaches that the atoning death of Jesus Christ avails for our sicknesses as well as for our sins; or, in other words, that "physical healing is in the atonement." I think that is a fair inference from these verses when looked at in their context.

This then raises another thorny issue that must be addressed: does the atonement guarantee healing for all?

Again, we will turn to the Isaiah 53 passage, which states in verse 5, "By His scourging [or stripes] we are healed." First Peter 2:24 quotes this text, and it is often used in support of the position that if our sin is completely healed at the cross, then our physical disease is as well. This would mean that the atonement is healing for all people all the time if they have faith to believe for it. Stated that simply, it certainly sounds great, but the context of 1 Peter 2:21–25 is clearly dealing with the issue of sin and not physical healing:

> You have been called for this purpose, since Christ also suffered for you, leaving you an example for you to follow in His steps, who committed no sin, nor was any deceit found in His mouth; and while being reviled, He did not revile in return; while suffering, He uttered no threats, but kept entrusting Himself to Him who judges righteously; and He Himself bore our sins in His body on the cross, so that we might die to sin and live to righteousness; for by His wounds you were healed. For you were continually straying like sheep, but now you have returned to the Shepherd and Guardian of your souls.

Verse 24 clearly states that "He Himself bore our sins in His body on the cross, so that we might die to sin and live to righteousness," so to declare that the atonement holds healing for all people all the time on the basis of these verses is certainly a misrepresentation of this scripture.

To take the position that the atonement holds a healing guarantee for all violates the whole of Scripture, which clearly teaches that the fullness of the kingdom and the wholeness of resurrection life are yet to come.

Revelation declares that there will be a day at the end of time when "He will wipe away every tear from their eyes; and there will no longer be any death; there will no longer be any mourning, or crying, or pain; the first things have passed away" (Rev. 21:4; see also Rom. 8:16–25; 2 Cor. 5:1–5; Rev. 21).

Declaring that the atonement is a guarantee of physical healing dangerously presumes on God and leaves no room for His sovereignty. Furthermore, though the atonement holds healing and though healing comes through the atonement, the promise of the atonement is not physical healing but forgiveness of sins. That is, our souls are completely saved in this age and all our sin forgiven, but our bodies will not experience the fullness of the kingdom of God until the age to come:

> We will all be changed, in a moment, in the twinkling of an eye, at the last trumpet; for the trumpet will sound, and the dead will be raised imperishable, and we will be changed. For this perishable must put on the imperishable, and this mortal must put on immortality. But when this perishable will have put on the imperishable, and this mortal will have put on immortality, then will come about the saying that is written, "Death is swallowed up in victory. O death, where is your victory? O death, where is your sting?" (1 Cor. 15:51–55)

In summary, we are living, as George Ladd has said, between the first and second comings of Christ, which places us, in Ladd's words, "in the now and not yet of the kingdom." God's part is releasing His power, authority and kingdom to bring healing to our hearts and lives. Our part is to believe and pray for His kingdom to come and His will to be done in every situation and then to trust Him, no matter the outcome.

Disease and Illness in Biblical Leaders

If the atonement were a guarantee of healing for all people all the time, then we would have serious reason to doubt the apostle Paul's ministry, which according to Galatians 4:13 included a serious bodily ailment: "You know that it was because of a bodily illness that I preached the gospel to you the first time."

Paul is just one of many New Testament leaders who struggled with sickness and disease. He says, "Trophimus I left sick at Miletus" (2 Tim. 4:20), and regarding poor Timothy, who it seems was often sick, we are told that Paul instructed him, "No longer drink water exclusively, but use a little wine for the sake of your stomach and your frequent ailments" (1 Tim. 5:23).

It is unmistakable here that Paul affirms the use of wine to help with Timothy's frequent stomach ailments. He doesn't say, "I am praying for your healing," or, "I am believing that you will have faith to receive your healing," or, "If you repent, God will heal you," or, "Please quit talking about your sickness and making negative declarations, and God will heal you." He simply states that God has made a natural way for Timothy to get some relief, namely, to take some wine, or, as we might say today, to go to the doctor. Paul obviously didn't think that this action would be interpreted as unspiritual.

It is important to note that Paul, Trophimus and Timothy were all highly esteemed leaders in ministry. They were mature believers who were not healed, as far as we know. Explanations for their continued illness such as personal sin or unbelief or unbelief in the people who prayed for them are simply not plausible here. Paul continued his ministry and continued to see others healed in his ministry, though it appears that he was not healed.

God's Heart for Healing

What the Word does teach is that there is healing in the atonement, healing for both sin and sickness, which I believe clearly makes it possible to state that God wants to heal people, all people, all the time. Please let me explain. He wants perfect health for us as much as He wants a sin-free world. But that will not happen this side of heaven, any more than all people will be healed from sin this side of heaven.

Those of us who live in God's grace and know His forgiveness for sin also know and are keenly aware that we still battle sin daily. Though we are forgiven, we are still living in a physical body and in a world that is in a battle. If Isaiah 53 is taken as it is given, Jesus clearly bore our sins on the cross, and by His stripes, or scourging, we are healed. We have no doubt that God wants to heal and forgive all sin for all people all the time. John 3:16 says so: "For God so loved the world, that He gave His only begotten Son, that whoever believes in Him shall not perish, but have eternal life."

So why do we doubt or fear to declare that likewise God wants to heal all people all the time? The answer is simple: because we see people we pray for not getting healed and at times even dying. So how could it be that God wants to heal all people all the time, unless, as some declare, it is a lack of faith that prevents some from being healed?

Simply put, sin and sickness were dealt with at the cross, but although we experience healing from sin daily, we are not yet completely healed from sin. And the same is true for physical healing. We can and do experience physical healing here on Earth, yet we will all ultimately die a physical death unless Jesus returns and takes us home first. We will not know perfect holiness this side of heaven, and likewise we will not know perfect health until we experience what Paul called "the redemption of our body" (Rom. 8:23).

We should pray for the sick as we pray for the lost, knowing that some will be saved, and some will be healed. Not all will be saved, and not all will be healed.

God simply doesn't heal all people all the time. Though we are told that Jesus healed all who were brought to Him (see Matt. 4:24;

8:16; Mark 1:32; Luke 6:18–19), we also see Jesus at the pool of Bethsaida, where sick people were lying about seeking physical healing, and we are told that Jesus healed only one man there (see John 5:1–9).

Barriers to Healing

Having stated that not all are healed, it is vital to discuss barriers to healing, for there are several. Earlier I mentioned that some people believe that a lack of faith is an issue that may prevent a physical healing. It is important to clarify this. All healing ministry is founded on faith. Without faith, the writer of Hebrews tells us, it is impossible to please God (see 11:6). Matthew 17:14–21 holds a story of Jesus painfully and passionately healing a boy:

> When they came to the crowd, a man came up to Jesus, falling on his knees before Him and saying, "Lord, have mercy on my son, for he is a lunatic and is very ill; for he often falls into the fire and often into the water. I brought him to Your disciples, and they could not cure him." And Jesus answered and said, "You unbelieving and perverted generation, how long shall I be with you? How long shall I put up with you? Bring him here to Me." And Jesus rebuked him, and the demon came out of him, and the boy was cured at once.
>
> Then the disciples came to Jesus privately and said, "Why could we not drive it out?" And He said to them, "Because of the littleness of your faith; for truly I say to you, if you have faith the size of a mustard seed, you will say to this mountain, 'Move from here to there,' and it will move; and nothing will be impossible to you. But this kind does not go out except by prayer and fasting."

Jesus' answer to the disciples' question unveils a barrier to healing: a littleness of faith, or a smallness of faith, as well as a lack of clear understanding regarding the demonic realm and the power of prayer and fasting. The change in Jesus' disciples after Pentecost is noteworthy if for no other reason than that it demonstrates how much their faith had grown. Peter and John healed a lame man in Acts 3:6, and Peter later tells the crowd,

> On the basis of faith in His name, it is the name of Jesus which has strengthened this man whom you see and know; and the faith which comes through Him has given him this perfect health in the presence of you all. (3:16)

The faith that comes through Jesus gave this man perfect health. So faith is crucial to healing, and a lack of faith can certainly be a barrier to God's will to heal. But it is important to note that it is not clear whose faith was at work here—the lame man's, the apostles or both. Since the faith was placed in Jesus, we can assume that it was likely John and Peter's faith that is principally referenced here.

Personal sin is another barrier to God's healing power. When a person chooses to willfully live in sin, that decision becomes an impediment to that person's healing. Following on the heels of James 5:14's directive to ask for healing prayer if we are sick, James 5:16 reminds us how sin can derail the very healing we seek: "Therefore, confess your sins to one another, and pray for one another so that you may be healed." Jesus is very clear in Mark 11:24–26 that unconfessed sin, and particularly an unforgiving and bitter spirit, hinders our prayers and our healing:

> Therefore I say to you, all things for which you pray and ask, believe that you have received them, and they will be granted you. Whenever you stand

praying, forgive, if you have anything against anyone, so that your Father who is in heaven will also forgive you your transgressions. But if you do not forgive, neither will your Father who is in heaven forgive your transgressions.

Further barriers to healing, fear and despair, go beyond unbelief, as does as a complete lack of faith for healing. These all impede the ability to pray with faith for healing.

Finally, many people are not healed because those praying expect an instant response, and when they don't get one, they quit praying. Those who persevere, however, are often the blessed recipients of the miracle they are seeking. Always continue to seek, ask and knock on the Father's heart until the Holy Spirit has released you to stop asking (see Luke 11:1–13).

Practical Issues of Healing Prayer

Praying for the sick provides a wonderful opportunity for both you and the ill person to grow. Often our first response to the Holy Spirit prompting us to pray for those who are sick is, "No way. I'll look like a fool! And God, what if You don't show up? What if You don't do anything?" The reality is that almost any time we pray for the sick, those we pray for are blessed and encouraged, whether they are immediately healed or not.

At Water of Life, we follow the biblical pattern found throughout the Word of laying on of hands while praying for the sick. There are multiple pictures of Jesus doing this in the New Testament (see Mark 5:23; 6:5; 8:23–25; 10:16; Luke 4:40; 13:13), and the apostles followed Jesus' example (see Acts 6:6; 8:17–19; 9:12, 17; 13:3).

We also often anoint a person with oil before praying. This oil represents the working and touch of the Holy Spirit. This too is a biblical thing to do:

Is anyone among you sick? Then he must call for the elders of the church and they are to pray over him, anointing him with oil in the name of the Lord; and the prayer offered in faith will restore the one who is sick, and the Lord will raise him up, and if he has committed sins, they will be forgiven him. (James 5:14–15)

Conclusion

In conclusion, it is important to remember that of the nine spiritual gifts listed in 1 Corinthians 12, only one is plural: the gifts of healing. It is not the *gift* of healing, implying that a person who employs this gift is now a healer. It is *gifts* of healing, which means that the one who is used to heal others only delivers the gift—he does not *have* it! I like to say that a person whom God uses to heal others is an errand boy! No one person is the healer who has the gift of healing. God gives us *gifts* of healing. We can all have these gifts, and we should all use them.

For additional resources on the topic of the Holy Spirit, listen to or view the sermon series "The Word and the Spirit" (available online at http://www.wateroflifecc.org/media#series_8 or on CD or DVD).

Women in Leadership in the Church

A Historical Look

Any attempt to tackle the topic of women in church leadership will meet with resistance at some level. This issue is massively misunderstood and has historically suffered from poor insight and bias. We will walk slowly and deeply into the fray that this issue of women and their place in ministry creates, believing that God has a clear path for us to follow, even if the journey is rough.

Before we embark on a look at the role of women in the church, we must do a historical review of the roles of both men and women, as these historical precedents tremendously impact our views on women in ministry. Genesis 5:1–2 is an appropriate place to begin:

> In the day when God created man, He made him in the likeness of God. He created them male and female, and He blessed them and named them Man in the day when they were created.

A clear historical view of men and women in Scripture will go a long way toward giving us a biblical understanding of the issue as it is dealt with in the New Testament. At the outset, it is important for us to note that God named both men and women *Adam*. Verse 2 states that they were named "Man," the Hebrew word used in verse 1 that is often translated *Adam*. In both cases the word is the Hebrew word *Adam*. It can be used for generic man or for the specific person Adam.

Genesis 2 gives a more specific account of creation and is often quoted in relation to men and women. In fact, when it is quoted in Ephesians 5:31, it becomes clear that God's original intent in Genesis 2 is still His redemptive plan in the New Testament.

Genesis 3 introduces us to the text that describes what is generally known as the fall of man. We meet face to face the horrendous curse that entered into humanity through the disobedience of Adam and Eve: man's lost authority and the entry of death into the world. After the pronouncement of the curse in Genesis 3:14–19, a seemingly innocuous statement is made: "Now the man called his wife's name Eve, because she was the mother of all the living" (3:20).

It is very important to note that this was the first time that women hadn't been called Adam. Eve had not had a name before the fall of man. Both she and Adam had been named Adam. Until the Fall they'd had one identity. She'd had a generic term that had defined her, the name *woman* in Genesis 2:22, but Adam and Eve's oneness was so complete that they had shared one name, *Adam*. The devastation of the Fall was monumental. Identity was lost, hope was lost, balance was lost, life was lost, and intimacy was lost. In summary, the curse was total and devastating.

For the woman the curse brought the pain of childbirth and the strain of a desire for a co-ruling position that she had lost. Genesis 3:16 clearly states her situation: "To the woman He said, 'I will greatly multiply your pain in childbirth, in pain you will bring forth children; yet your desire will be for your husband, and he will rule over you.'"

This statement "your desire" is the word *teshuqah*. It means "to desire," "to long for," "to crave something." In this case, the woman's desire would be for position. The curse had effectually destroyed the intimate and balanced roles of men and women. Now there would be a hungering desire on the woman's part to return to that co-ruling position with man. This is not a judgment on the skill or ability of women; it is a reality of the curse.

The last part of verse 16 declares, "And he will rule over you" (*rule* comes from *mashal*, "oversight"). This oversight that the curse ushered in does not carry the connotation of men bossing women around because they are the king of the castle. This authority conferred on man as leader was to be directed by clear and thoughtful boundaries. Redeeming boundaries, such as those seen in Ephesians 5:23–25:

> The husband is the head of the wife, as Christ also is the head of the church, He Himself being the Savior of the body. But as the church is subject to Christ, so also the wives ought to be to their husbands in everything. Husbands, love your wives, just as Christ also loved the church and gave Himself up for her.

There would be authority, and there would be submission. Any time there is authority, there will be submission issues. Men have abused authority, and women long for their intended role as co-leader.

Men are directed to love their wives as Christ loved the church. If we followed Christ's example, our wives would struggle with very little. Jesus' love for the church and for people positions Him more than any person who ever walked the planet to understand people's need for redemption and for redemptive values.

Clearly there would be strife after the Fall, and there had to be a head, a leader. This does not indicate inferiority of women or superiority of man, but it does imply a functional difference in roles. There is no reflection on skills or gifts here. Also, the Bible does not teach a subservient role for woman in regard to man in general, but rather the roles are clearly defined as those between husband and wife. A quick look at 1 Peter 3:5–7 affirms these roles:

> In this way in former times the holy women also, who hoped in God, used to adorn themselves, being submissive to their own husbands; just as Sarah obeyed Abraham, calling him lord, and you have become her children if you do what is right without being frightened by any fear.
>
> You husbands in the same way, live with your wives in an understanding way, as with someone weaker, since she is a woman; and show her honor as a fellow heir of the grace of life, so that your prayers will not be hindered.

A Redemptive Plan

The cross was meant to deliver us into a redemptive plan that would restore us and continue to redeem us from the curse in an ongoing fashion. Second Corinthians 1:10 makes this clear: God "delivered us from so great a peril of death, and will deliver us, He on whom we have set our hope. And He will yet deliver us."

Many reject any Old Testament reference concerning the role of women in the church as biased and unjust due to the prevailing patriarchal atmosphere of early biblical times. But the Old Testament view of women must be tempered with the heart that God revealed through Jesus toward women. Much that had grown out of the Old Testament needed clarifying and restoring when Jesus arrived on the scene, and He immediately set about challenging and dismantling a broken and contrived system that the Pharisees had used to enslave people (see the Beatitudes and the Sermon on the Mount, Matt. 5–7).

New Testament

One of the things Jesus did often and did well was to challenge the status of women. Take a brief look at Jesus' ministry with women, since He obviously sets the pace for the role of women in the New Testament church:

> Jesus broke rabbinical tradition and talked with women, including a Samaritan woman (see John 4:7).
> He healed women (see Luke 13:10–12).
> He taught them (see Luke 10:38–42).
> He defended their right to be taught (see Luke 10:42).
> He included them in parables (see Matt. 13:33).
> He allowed them to travel with Him (see Luke 8:1–2).

Jesus broke tradition in His ministry to and with women, offering women the self-worth they are due. Yet He did not call any women as apostles (see Matt. 10:2–4), nor did He send women out to preach, teach or heal (see Matt. 10:1–42).

Old Testament

The role of women in the Old Testament church was interesting and complex. Women were expected at the three major feasts (see Deut. 16:11, 14). Peninnah took a portion to sacrifice and to seek forgiveness for sin (see 1 Sam. 1:4). This we know: women participated in worship services at some level. Leviticus 12 outlines the sacrifices a woman should offer after giving birth, and even though only priests could go inside the temple, women ministered (*tsaba*, "serve in the army" or "service"; this same word is used for Levitical priests in Numbers 4:23) at the door of the tent of meeting (see Exod. 38:8; 1 Sam. 2:22). This seemed to be a regular ongoing ministry, "possibly of prayer."[1] A woman could take the vow of a Nazirite to separate herself to the Lord just as a man could (see Num. 6:1–21). Women participated during the teaching and reading of the Law, according to Deuteronomy 31:12: "Assemble the people, the men and the women and children and the alien who is in your town, so that they may hear and learn and fear the LORD your God, and be careful to observe all the words of this law." Women could also pray without the assistance of a priest (see Gen. 16:7–13). These details show that women had more than a passing role in the Old Testament church and worship services.

We also know that women held places of leadership in the Old Testament, both in government and in the service of the temple. Deborah was a prophetess (*nebiah*, from *nabi*, "authorized spokesman") who "was judging Israel" (see Judg. 4:4), and Miriam, Huldah and Noadiah were prophetesses as well (see Exod. 15:20; 2 Kings 22:14; Neh. 6:14). Some Old Testament women were called wise (*chakam*, see 2 Sam. 14:2) as well as industrious and active (see Prov. 31:10–31).

We see that the Old Testament woman was involved in learning the Law, sacrificing to receive cleansing from sin, serving at the church (the tent of meeting), prophesying and praying as well as serving in government, judging Israel. Before leaving the Old Testament, however, we should also note that women are not seen as priests, teachers or readers of the Law.

Early Church

As we move to the early church, the role of women begins to come into focus as we find several things:

> Women joined with men in praying in the Upper Room at Pentecost (see Acts 1:14).
> Women received the gifts of the Spirit (see 1 Cor. 12:7).
> Women received Christ and were baptized (see Acts 5:14; 8:12).
> Women were persecuted (see Acts 9:2).
> Women were prophetesses (see Acts 21:9).
> Women were teachers—Priscilla and her husband

Aquila "explained" [*ektithémi*, "anointed," "set forth"] the way of God to Apollos (see Acts 18:26). Women were called fellow workers (see Phil. 4:3). Finally, women were leaders in the early church in the role of deacons (see Rom. 16:1).

Problem Texts

This discussion is fraught with difficult and often misunderstood texts that must be addressed to clarify New Testament purpose and ministry direction for women. It is crucial as we look into this issue that we remember the outcome of the curse and its effect on the role of women as it pertains to ruling and leading. Woman has always lived with a natural desire to lead. She was created to lead, and she shared leadership with Adam prior to the Fall. That natural desire comes into play in the formulation of many of the New Testament texts concerning women and ministry, particularly when these texts are offering a framework that promotes God's redemptive plan for women.

1 Corinthians 11

Beginning our review of these difficult texts in 1 Corinthians 11:3–15, we see that Paul outlines two key issues: headship and head coverings. In verse 3 he says, "Christ is the head of every man, and the man [*anér*] is the head [*kephalé*] of a woman." Paul uses this term *anér* often, and how it is translated is crucial to any and every discussion pertaining to women and ministry.

Anér is used fifteen times in 1 Corinthians 7, and it is translated "husband" each time, not "man." The word is used commonly for both husband and man; the King James Version translates it "husband" thirty-four out of the fifty-nine times it is used in the New Testament, and eighteen of the remaining twenty-five times a cursory review reveals that it appears to reference husbands, even though it is translated "man." That leaves seven times that it is clearly used for man or men.

It is important to note this, as it is entirely possible that the husband was being referenced in some of Paul's texts in which we have translated *anér* in different versions as "man" or "men." This change directly impacts what the author is communicating. An obvious instance is at hand here in verse 3. If *anér* is referencing *husband*, then the husband is the head of his wife. If it is *men* or *man*, then men are the head of women.

As to this text clarifying women and their role in ministry, 1 Corinthians 11:5 certainly gives credence to the fact that women can and do minister in public gatherings, or in the local church. They obviously do have a say—the ability and position to speak during a service—since verse 5 states, "Every woman who has her head uncovered while praying or prophesying disgraces her head." What this covering is isn't exactly clear, though I believe Paul was speaking of her hair. What *is* clear here is that New Testament women prayed and prophesied in public meetings—in the local church.

1 Corinthians 14

First Corinthians 11:5, however, seems to fly in the face of texts exhorting women to keep quiet in church. These texts obviously cannot mean that she can never speak, since she is allowed to pray and prophesy. The context of 1 Corinthians 11 is the public meeting of the church, so how can what is said there be reconciled with 1 Corinthians 14:34–35:

> The women are to keep silent in the churches; for they are not permitted to speak, but are to subject themselves, just as the Law also says. If they desire to learn anything, let them ask their own husbands at home; for it is improper for a woman to speak in church.

Before we answer this question, a quick historical look at Acts 1 and 2 would be in order. Acts 1:14 tells us that women were present at the meeting in the Upper Room: "These all with one mind were continually devoting themselves to prayer, along with the women, and Mary the mother of Jesus, and with His brothers." After the Spirit was poured out in Acts 2, Peter began to defend what had taken place; he quoted from Joel 2, which clearly includes women prophesying, so it is again apparent that women are gifted with public ministry gifts.

It is sufficiently clear that women would function in public ministry in the newly birthed church. We know that such ministry actively took place in the New Testament church when we read of Philip's four daughters in Acts 21:9, who were prophetesses. Thus any declaration that women cannot speak or lead in church can and should be challenged. It is abundantly clear that women led in the Old Testament, with Deborah, Miriam and others previously mentioned. Furthermore, 2 Corinthians 3:7–8 declares that the glory of the New Testament surpasses the glory of the old covenant, so it would certainly stand to reason that women would have an even greater role in New Testament ministry than they did in the Old Testament.

Phoebe is an example of this. We find her mentioned in Romans 16:1–2, defined in terms of leadership as she is commended by Paul:

> I commend to you our sister Phoebe, who is a servant of the church which is at Cenchrea; that you receive her in the Lord in a manner worthy of the saints, and that you help her in whatever matter she may have need of you; for she herself has also been a helper of many, and of myself as well.

Phoebe is referred to first as our sister, so we know that she is female. But Paul also refers to her as "a servant [*diakonos*, "servant," "minister," "bearer of a specific office," "deacon"] of the church which is at Cenchrea." This function of deacon is a leading role of significance. First Timothy 3:11 confirms this leadership office for women.

1 Timothy 3

The context of 1 Timothy 3 is important here. Verse 11, in the original language, can refer either to wives or to women in general. Some feel that the passage refers to deacons' wives rather than to women deacons, since in the preceding verse Paul was addressing deacons. The New King James Version seems to indicate this: "Let them serve as deacons, being found blameless. Likewise, their wives must be reverent, not slanderers, temperate, faithful in all things" (3:10–11). But if this passage is referring to deacon's wives, why is there not a similar exhortation concerning elders' wives in verses 1–7, since the office of elder is the highest office and more important than that of deacon?

In verse 8, when moving from instruction to elders to instruction to deacons, Paul introduces a break in the text: "Deacons likewise must be men of dignity." It seems clear that after his instruction to deacons, Paul introduces a similar break in verse 11 to introduce the office for women, which is more clearly seen in the New American Standard Bible: "Women must likewise be dignified." This is an obvious reference to the office at hand.

Reconciling Problem Passages

How then do we reconcile the role of women in leadership in the church with the two most confining texts declaring that women must remain silent in the church—those found in 1 Corinthians 14:35 and 1 Timothy 2:11–12? First we will explore the wording in 1 Corinthians 14:34–35, where instruction is given by Paul:

The women are to keep silent in the churches; for they are not permitted to speak, but are to subject themselves, just as the Law also says. If they desire to learn anything, let them ask their own husbands at home; for it is improper for a woman to speak in church.

There are a couple of key textual insights that come into play here. First is the word *silent*, or *sigaó*; this word is used by Paul in this chapter in verse 28 when he is addressing speaking in tongues in the church. One of the standing rules of Bible interpretation, also known as hermeneutics, is to if at all possible allow the Bible to interpret itself, finding another use of the word we are studying and examining the context in which it is used. This is particularly true if the word is used by the same author in the same context, passage or book.

Fortunately, that is exactly the scenario we have in the case of the word *silent*, or *sigaó*. If we want to know exactly what Paul meant by telling women to remain silent, we need to look at Paul's intent in verse 28. Does the command to keep silent in the service if there is no interpreter mean that the believers should never speak in tongues? No, it is quite obvious from verse 27 that tongues speaking was to go on when an interpreter was present; the Greek lexicon's definition of *sigaó* supports this position, defining *sigaó* as "to hold one's peace."

The emphasis of the word is not on an external command to remain quiet but on an internal decision to hold one's peace. What does this mean for women? They need to hang back, hold back and allow men to speak and lead. Restraint is the sense this passage gives. This has to do with the intuitive desire that women have to move and speak into spiritual matters in an initiating fashion. This is the struggle of the curse previously mentioned.

Church history tells us that early church sermons may have consisted of question-and-answer discussions. We see, for example, that when Paul and a group of believers "were gathered together to break bread, Paul began talking [*dielegeto*, "conversed," "reasoned"] to them" (Acts 20:7). As such, the services would have been ordered and peaceful. That is why 1 Corinthians 14:35 fits this context: "Let them ask their own husbands at home."

First Timothy 2:8–15 would also support this framework. In verse 8 Paul instructs the men in proper worship, addressing their heart attitude as vital as he instructs them to pray "without wrath and dissension." In verses 11 and 12, he does the same for women, stating, "A woman must quietly [*hesychia*, "quietness," "to not meddle"] receive instruction [*manthanó*, "to learn, be instructed"] with entire [*pas*, "complete," "all"] submissiveness" (*hupotagé*, "subordinating herself in every respect"; usually a military term meaning "rank under"[2]).

In verse 12 Paul elaborates, "I do not allow [*epitrepó*, "to permit"; present tense emphasizes the continual action and points to an abiding attitude[3]] a woman to teach" (*didaskein*, "to teach." Aorist tense could have been used here to denote simple action, but "present infin. indicates a condition or process. This *didaxai* [aorist] is to teach, while *didaskein* [present vs. 2:12], is to be a teacher"[4]). So Paul is stating that a woman is not to be a teacher "or exercise authority [*authenteó*, "to be dominating," "to execute one's own hand or will"] over a man [*anér*], but to remain quiet."

Or is that what he is saying?

Again we confront this term *anér*. Was Paul directing women to hold back and to remain quiet, to not exercise authority over or to teach their husbands—or was this discourse referencing men in general? Was Paul saying that a wife shouldn't be the spiritual leader of the home, teaching her husband? Or was he stating a fundamental spiritual truth that all women had to submit to all men?

The word that seems to hold the key to Paul's context here is found in verse 11 of 1 Timothy 2: *hesychia*, defined above as "quietness," is used in the text, declaring, "A woman must quietly receive instruction." Fortunately, this word—like *sigaó*, "silent," which we saw in 1 Corinthians 14—is used again by Paul in the same context, passage and book. Only ten verses prior, in 1 Timothy 2:2, Paul states that the believers should pray "for kings and all who are in authority, so that we may lead a tranquil and quiet life in all godliness and dignity."

The word translated "quiet" is the same word, *hesychia*. What is Paul saying? "Intercede and pray so that no one can speak and we can lead a tranquil and peaceable life," makes no sense in this context. Paul is communicating the need to be in prayer for leaders in order to bring about a peaceable land. The root of this word means "to sit" or "to be still or tranquil." Paul is saying, "Women, restrain your desire to lead and to take over the role of your husband." With this in mind, Paul isn't likely telling women that they can never speak. He is rather saying that women are to remain still and thoughtful, allowing men—*anér*, their husbands—to step out of their comfort zones and to initiate ministry, to lead. Clearly, the New Testament teaches that women are to submit to their husbands, but it never suggests that women in general are to submit to men.

A look at 1 Timothy 2:11–12 helps us with this:

> A woman must quietly receive instruction with entire submissiveness. But I do not allow a woman to teach or exercise authority over a man, but to remain quiet.

Using our understanding of the original language, an apt paraphrase of this passage might be,

> A woman must be still and allow her husband to lead. I don't allow a woman to teach or to disciple her husband, nor do I allow her to dominate or boss her husband around. She must restrain her spirit and let him lead.

Verses 13–14 support this context: "For it was Adam who was first created, and then Eve. And it was not Adam who was deceived, but the woman being deceived, fell into transgression." Remember here that Adam and Eve were the first husband and wife in creation. Women were cursed with the pain of childbearing and with a desire to be restored to the role of leadership that they lost. Both of these issues have been spoken to here and are addressed throughout Scripture, and they support the context of women submitting to their husbands, not to men in general.

Proverbs 9:13 addresses the state of a woman who doesn't want to restrain herself: "The woman of folly is boisterous, she is naive and knows nothing." First Peter 3:1–4 restates the need for women to restrain themselves in order to win an unbelieving husband, using the same word *hesychia*:

> You wives, be submissive to your own husbands so that even if any of them are disobedient to the word, they may be won without a word by the behavior of their wives, as they observe your chaste and respectful behavior. Your adornment must not be merely external—braiding the hair, and wearing gold jewelry, or putting on dresses; but let it be the hidden person of the heart, with the imperishable quality of a gentle and quiet spirit, which is precious in the sight of God.

God is obviously saying, "Women, your men need you to step back so that they can step up." Please buy into the program God has set up that allows men to flourish and fulfill their destiny, and God will do the same for you.

Notes

Women in Leadership in the Church

1. Susan T. Foh, *Women and the Word of God: A Response to Biblical Feminism* (Grand Rapids: Baker, 1979), 83.
2. W. E. Vine, *An Expository Dictionary of New Testament Words* (Grand Rapids: Zondervan, 1940), 86.
3. Fritz Rieneker, *Linguistic Key to the Greek New Testament* (Grand Rapids: Zondervan, 1976), 621.
4. H. E. Dana and Julius R. Mantey, *A Manual Grammar of the Greek New Testament* (London: MacMillan, 1957), 199.

Bibliography

The Ministry and Gift of Prophecy

Aland, Kurt, Matthew Black, Carlo M. Martini, Bruce M. Metzger, and Allen Wikgren, eds. *The Greek New Testament*. Stuttgart, Germany. Biblia-Druck, GmbH (German Bible Society), 1998.

Bromiley, Geoffrey W., Gerhard Kittle, Gerhard Friedrich, eds. *Theological Dictionary of the New Testament: Abridged in One Volume*. Grand Rapids. Eerdmans, 1985.

Brown, Colin, ed. *New International Dictionary of New Testament Theology*. Vols. 1, 2 and 3. Grand Rapids. Zondervan, 1979.

Easton, M. G. *Easton's Bible Dictionary*. CD-ROM. Logos Bible Software.

Harris, R. Laird, Gleason L. Archer, Bruce K. Walke. *Theological Wordbook of the Old Testament*. Vol. 2. Chicago. Moody, 1980.

Ladd, George Eldon. *A Theology of the New Testament*. Edited by Donald A. Hagner. Grand Rapids. Eerdmans, 1994.

Moulton, Harold K., ed. *The Analytical Greek Lexicon Revised*. Grand Rapids. Zondervan, 1977.

Thayer, Joseph Henry. *Thayer's Greek Definitions*. QuickVerse Bible Software. CD-ROM. Cedar Rapids, IA. Parsons Technology Inc., 1999.

Thomas, Robert L., ed. *New American Standard Exhaustive Concordance of the Bible: Hebrew-Aramaic and Greek Dictionaries*. CD-ROM. QuickVerse Bible Software. Cedar Rapids, IA. Parsons Technology, 1998.

Water of Life Community Church. *Ministry and Gifts of the Holy Spirit II*. Rancho Cucamonga, CA. Water of Life, 2009.

Williams, J. Rodney. *Renewal Theology: Systematic Theology from a Charismatic Perspective.* Grand Rapids. Zondervan, 1996.

Bibliography

Women in Leadership in the Church

Dana, H. E. and Julius R. Mantey. *A Manual Grammar of the Greek New Testament*. London. MacMillan, 1957.

Foh, Susan T. *Women and the Word of God: A Response to Biblical Feminism*. Grand Rapids. Baker, 1979.

Friberg, Barbara, Timothy Friberg, Kurt Aland, eds. *Analytical Greek New Testament*. Grand Rapids. Baker, 1981.

Green, J. P., Jr., ed. *The Interlinear Hebrew-Aramaic Old Testament*. Peabody, MA. Hendrickson, 1976.

Harris, R. Laird, Gleason L. Archer, Bruce K. Walke. *Theological Word book of the Old Testament*. 2 vols. Chicago. Moody, 1980.

Marshall, Alfred. *The NASB Interlinear Greek-English New Testament*. Grand Rapids. Zondervan, 1984.

Moulton, Harold K., ed. *The Analytical Greek Lexicon Revised*. Grand Rapids. Zondervan, 1977.

Rienecker, Fritz. *Linguistic Key to the Greek New Testament*. Grand Rapids. Zondervan, 1976.

Vine, W. E. *An Expository Dictionary of New Testament Words*. Grand Rapids. Zondervan, 1940.

Wigram, George V. and Ralph D. Winter. *The Word Study Concordance*. Wheaton. Tyndale, 1972.

About the Author

Dan Carroll grew up in Pomona, California. In February of 1970, he received Christ as his savior at a Youth for Christ meeting. In 1976 he received a B.A. in Religion from the University of La Verne and went on to teach in the Pomona Unified School District for three years. Then in 1979 he received his M.A. in Education from the Claremont Graduate University. Dan and his wife, Gale, moved to Idaho, where he taught high-school English and history and coached the basketball team. He also served as an elder at Community Fellowship Church.

In 1982 Dan took a youth-pastor position at Life Bible Fellowship in Upland, California, and served there until 1987. He received an M.A. in Christian Ministry from the International School of Theology in 1987.

In 1987 Pastor Dan began teaching a men's Bible study. For three years the study grew in scope and depth, and the families of the men involved began to come together for fellowship. In 1989 Dan and his family went to the Youth With A Mission training school in Kona, Hawaii. They were introduced to cross-cultural ministry in Penang, Malaysia, where Dan received a vision for the world. After returning to the United States in 1990, he was encouraged by the men of his Bible study and their families to plant a church. This became Water of Life Community Church.

Pastor Dan completed a Doctorate of Ministry from The King's Seminary in 2004. He continues today as the senior pastor of Water of Life Community Church.

Dan and Gale have been married for thirty-two years and have two adult children, Shane and Katie.

About Water of Life

Water of Life Community Church is a non-denominational evangelical charismatic church. This means that we are devoted to studying and obeying the Bible, which is the Word of God, and we believe in the baptism of the Holy Spirit and the modern-day operation of the gifts proclaimed in the New Testament.

Water of Life was established on Sunday, October 28, 1990, when a group of twenty-one adults and eleven children gathered together to worship at the La Petite Childcare building in Rancho Cucamonga, California. It was a fellowship that arose from a men's Bible study, a group of people who grew together, and a body that is now committed together to seek God's plan as a church family.

Many people love God but have become disillusioned with the church. Therefore, a church that offers a personal encounter with Jesus Christ and growth in His Word without the clutter of an overly structured environment has great appeal. Because we want to maintain the integrity and purity of our spiritual purpose, we do not have a rigorous structure with multitudes of committees or membership requirements.

Our desire is to walk by faith and in deep trust of our Lord. Consequently, you will not see us take an offering. Rather, we believe that the giving of tithes and offerings is worship to Jesus Christ and an expression of the relationship between each individual giver and the Lord.

Although Water of Life is a non-denominational church, we consider ourselves a church that is interdependent with the rest of the body of Christ. Our church is governed by our pastors and our elder board. Additionally, our senior pastor is accountable to an outside group of senior pastors from other local churches as well as to an internationally recognized leader from the Foursquare denomination.

Our Core Values

Healing

Healing is the very starting point of a transformed life. It speaks to maturing people into a closer relationship with Christ, not just to getting better inside. Jesus put a huge value on healing—putting people back together again. Healing of sick, wounded and broken lives is a high priority to a compassionate and loving God:

> The Spirit of the LORD is upon me, for he has anointed me to bring Good News to the poor. He has sent me to proclaim that captives will be released, that the blind will see, that the oppressed will be set free, and that the time of the LORD's favor has come. (Luke 4:18–19, NLT)

Healing is so important to God that He made it a key part of discipleship, or growing in Jesus. Healing occurred many times in Jesus' ministry, and miracles frequently occurred. But Jesus' healing was not just about making people well physically. Rather, it was to restore them in the kingdom of God, to bring them into a right relationship with God. Ephesians 4:11–13 talks of apostles, prophets, evangelists, pastors and teachers all having the responsibility "to equip God's people to do his work and build up the church, the body of Christ . . . until we all come to such unity in our faith and knowledge of God's Son that we will be mature in the Lord, measuring up to the full and complete standard of Christ" (4:12–13, NLT). The word *equip*, *kartatizo* in Greek, means "to mend, restore and be put back together."

> I will sprinkle clean water on you, and you will be clean. Your filth will be washed away, and you will no longer worship idols. And I will give you a new heart, and I will put a new spirit in you. I will take out your stony, stubborn heart and give you a tender, responsive heart. And I will put my Spirit in you so you will follow my decrees and be careful to obey my regulations. (Ezek. 36:25–27, NLT)

The goal in all we do must be transformation—that is where winning begins. God has called us into relationship with one another so that we can be healed and then become instruments of His healing.

> Blessed be the God and Father of our Lord Jesus Christ, the Father of mercies and God of all comfort, who comforts us in all our affliction so that we will be able to comfort those who are in any affliction with the comfort with which we ourselves are comforted by God. (2 Cor. 1:3–4)

God does not call us to store up what He gives us but to pass it on to others. Transformation occurs in our church's small groups as well as in our healing and recovery groups, in which people can find support, care, prayer and encouragement.

Sending

Sending is our second core value. We believe it is foundational to all that God wants to do in us.

Everything about us likes to be comfortable, *but Jesus told us that the way for us to grow is to be stretched out* (*ekteno* in the Greek). We need to get out of our comfort zones.

In Acts 13:1–3 we read that the church in Jerusalem sent Paul and Barnabas out on the first real missionary journey. Their goal was to reproduce the work God had done in them and in other believers by spreading the word of Jesus' love, transforming lives and starting churches. This church-planting model has been followed in various forms ever since. Our desire at Water of Life is to send teams out for short-term exposure on a regular basis and at the same time to train and expose our church to as many cross-cultural types of ministry as possible. This includes those near to us (in our valley) and those far from us (all over the world). In our history we have sent short-term teams to between fifteen and twenty different countries, including Malaysia, Hong Kong, Russia, China, Jamaica, Venezuela, Guatemala, Lebanon, Panama, Kenya, Nicaragua, El Salvador, Cuba and Honduras. More recently, we have sent teams to Mexico, Cambodia and Thailand.

Jesus told His disciples in Matthew 28:19, "Go therefore and make disciples of all the nations, baptizing them in the name of the Father and the Son and the Holy Spirit." In Acts 1:4–8 He told them more:

> Gathering them together, He commanded them not to leave Jerusalem, but to wait for what the Father had promised, "Which," He said, "you heard of from Me; for John baptized with water, but you will be baptized with the Holy Spirit not many days from now." So when they had come together, they were asking Him, saying, "Lord, is it at this time You are restoring the kingdom to Israel?" He said to them, "It is not for you to know times or epochs which the Father has fixed by His own authority; but you will receive power when the Holy Spirit has come upon you; and you shall be My witnesses both in Jerusalem, and in all Judea and Samaria, and even to the remotest part of the earth.

Jerusalem and Judea were home to Jesus and the disciples—that is, local. So we likewise do local outreach at our food-and-clothing warehouse, at Adopt-a-Block, at Mobile Medical Unit and with our annual Trunk-or-Treat Halloween-alternative event. The remote parts of the world for Water of Life are Cambodia and Thailand as well as other nations we have reached. This outreach is all based on Holy Spirit empowerment, and we seek to establish long-term relationships in each of these areas. This will result in transformed lives—in us as we go and in others as they receive.

Equipping

> And He gave some as apostles, and some as prophets, and some as evangelists, and some as pastors and teachers, for the equipping of the saints for the work of service, to the building up of the body of Christ. (Eph. 4:11–12)

This core value, like the ones before it, speaks to transforming lives. At Water of Life *winning* is defined as "a transformed life demonstrated by a person being given to God and given to other people." In regard to equipping, as we at Water of Life learn the truth in the Word of God, we receive training along with it as to what we are to do with what we learn. Following God is not just about words—it is an action. A changed person is one who loves God and loves people as well as serves God and serves people.

Equipping at Water of Life means more than just attending church or a Bible study: "The things which you have heard from me in the presence of many witnesses, entrust these to faithful men who will be able to teach others also" (2 Tim. 2:2).

At Water of Life, equipping means teaching and releasing people with the purpose of both mind transformation and heart transformation. Practically speaking, all our small groups will teach and do outreach ministry in which they extend themselves to others. Individuals as well are provided with the opportunity to serve by caring for others—putting their knowledge to work to give life to other people.

Caring

> What use is it, my brethren, if someone says he has faith but has no works? Can that faith save him? If a brother or sister is without clothing and in need of daily food, and one of you says to them, "Go in peace, be warmed and be filled," and yet you do not give them what is necessary for their body, what use is that? Even so faith, if it has no works, is dead, being by itself. (James 2:14–17)

We believe that one of Water of Life's main priorities is to care for those in need. The principle is this: we get so we can give. We believe this is a part of God's heart for all people. We need the poor and downtrodden as much as they need us. It is through them that we gain the heart of God and the Holy Spirit is able to soften us and impart the Father's heart to us.

The Bible is emphatic about the church's responsibility to care for those in need: "But whoever has the world's goods, and sees his brother [or sister] in need and closes his heart against him, how does the love of God abide in him?" (1 John 3:17).

In Matthew 25 we read that Jesus expects nothing less from His church, which is why this core value is so important at Water of Life.

This expectation is clearly shown in Scripture:

> Then the King will say to those on His right, "Come, you who are blessed of My Father, inherit the kingdom prepared for you from the foundation of the world. For I was hungry, and you gave Me something to eat; I was thirsty, and you gave Me something to drink; I was a stranger, and you invited Me in; naked, and you clothed Me; I was sick, and you visited Me; I was in prison, and you came to Me." (Matt. 25:34–36)

We want to be counted among the faithful described above as those who fed the hungry, gave drink to the thirsty, invited the stranger in, clothed the naked, cared for the sick and also visited those in prison. "The King will answer and say to them, 'Truly I say to you, to the extent that you did it to one of these brothers of Mine, even the least of them, you did it to Me'" (Matt. 25:40).

Relationships

Lives are transformed through relationships—community and family relationships: "You are citizens along with all of God's holy people. You are members of God's family. . . . We [who believe] are carefully joined together in him, becoming a holy temple for the Lord" (Eph. 2:19, 21, NLT).

Everyone who believes in Jesus is part of His family. He has joined us together, and He tells us that we should get along. He is the One who holds everything together. He holds the world together, He holds marriages together, He holds the church family together and He holds personal relationships together: "He is before all things, and in Him all things hold together" (Col. 1:17).

First Corinthians is quite clear in telling us that He put all of us together; we are one body, and we are supposed to live as if we are:

> For even as the body is one and yet has many members, and all the members of the body, though they are many, are one body, so also is Christ. For by one Spirit we were all baptized into one body, whether Jews or Greeks, whether slaves or free, and we were all made to drink of one Spirit. (1 Cor. 12:12–13)

The rules of the family of God are clear and simple: we are called to serve one another. This is only possible through our relationship with Jesus. To have a powerful and on-fire relationship with Jesus, we have to get our mind off ourselves and choose to focus on other people. Christ always did this. He built His relationships with many people based on compassion, and He asks us to do the same. In Mark 1:41, as Jesus spoke with a leper, He was "moved with compassion." He stretched out His hand, touched the leper and healed him. In order for us to be really connected with others at a deep level, we must be compassionate.

The heart of a servant is a heart of compassion. There is power in serving others, and there is also blessing in serving others. As we come together in right relationship with other people, we position ourselves to be blessed by God.

Contact us at:

Water of Life Community Church
7625 East Avenue, Fontana, CA, 92336

Water of Life Administration Office
14418 Miller Avenue, Suite K, Fontana, CA 92336

Phone: 909.463.0103
Fax: 909.463.1436
E-mail: info@wateroflifecc.org

Made in the USA
San Bernardino, CA
01 November 2017